EAST ANGLIA
IN PHOTOGRAPHS

JAMIE SKIPPER

AMBERLEY

First published 2019

Amberley Publishing
The Hill, Stroud
Gloucestershire, GL5 4EP

www.amberley-books.com

Copyright © Jamie Skipper, 2019

The right of Jamie Skipper to be identified as the Author of this work has been
asserted in accordance with the Copyrights, Designs and Patents Act 1988.

ISBN 978 1 4456 8836 7 (print)
ISBN 978 1 4456 8837 4 (ebook)

British Library Cataloguing in Publication Data.
A catalogue record for this book is available from the British Library.

Typesetting by Aura Technology and Software Services, India.
Printed in the UK.

ACKNOWLEDGEMENTS

First off, I'd like to thank my mum, Janice, for the support and encouragement through the years and my late father, Phillip, from whom I gained my love of photography and who had cameras for a long as I can remember. To my younger brother, Chris, who shares my interest in photography and is quite a good photographer in his own way, plus was useful for ideas for destinations for the book. Thanks also to my older brother, Gary.

Thanks also to my great friend Marisha Haylett, who always has good things to say about my work, even when I'm not so sure.

I also have to thank Marcus Tilsley, who talked me into going ahead with the first book, and again to Rod Gowen, whose interest in photography is handy when I need ideas or fascinating chats about it. Thanks also to Martin Cameron, whose artistic side has always been an inspiration to me over the years, and to my work colleagues Owen Gedge, Brandon Dade, Michael Walker and Sydney Gedge for their support. And finally, to my neighbour Jackie Parkinson, who has put up with noise at unearthly hours next door.

At Amberley Publishing, thanks to Alan Murphy, who saw my work and gave me the opportunity to produce my first book. Also to Jenny Stephens, the local history team's managing editor, who bridged the gap between me and Amberley. Also at Amberley: Nick Grant, Nikki Embery, Becky Cousins and Sarah Greenwood.

Thanks also to Canon for their great cameras. I have used them for years; in fact they are the only manufacturer of DSLR I've used. Also thanks to my local camera store WEX, with their great selection of gear and as it's just five minutes away, it is very handy – I've spent thousands there over the years.

Thanks also to all my followers on Instagram, Flickr, Twitter and Facebook, whose likes, comments and follows are very much appreciated and inspire me to get out and produce more images.

And last but not least, thanks must be given to all the people who purchased my first book, *Norfolk in Photographs*. You have my deepest appreciation and gratitude.

ABOUT THE PHOTOGRAPHER

Jamie Skipper is a self-taught amateur photographer, born and bred in the lovely county of Norfolk where much of his landscape photography has been taken. It is here he spends time enjoying the early sunrises and warm sunset, taking in the fresh air, walking along the quiet beaches and waterways in the early pre-dawn or twilight while most people are still in bed as he waits for the exquisite light that only the golden hours of dawn and dusk can produce. Beautiful oranges, blues, pinks and purples, lost in the full sunlight of the later day ahead, can be fully apricated in the remote landscapes around the county, with only the birds singing, deer and foxes roaming the countryside and if you're lucky a barn owl silently quartering a meadow for company, making for a peaceful relaxing experience far away from the bustle of everyday life.

Using exclusively Canon gear, starting in the relatively distant past with a film Canon EOS 550n and working through several digital models, Jamie currently uses Canon's Full Frame EOS 6D with a range of their superbly built and pin-sharp L lenses, which perform very well and will last for years. He has also started to use Lee Filters. His favourite is the 10 stop filter, which turns even daylight shots into dramatic cloud, blurring long exposures that really transform the image.

Website: www.jdsphoto.co.uk
Instagram: jamie_skipper_photography
Twitter: twitter.com/JDS9_Photo
Facebook: www.facebook.com/JamieSkipperPhotography

INTRODUCTION

Sitting in the east of Great Britain is the beautiful area known as East Anglia, a quiet corner of the country comprising Norfolk, Suffolk and Cambridgeshire. It is full of stunning landscapes and history, with the ancient cities of Norwich, Cambridge, Ely and Peterborough and their magnificent cathedrals, and the historic Ipswich in Suffolk, on the River Orwell.

The three counties offer a multitude of different landscapes: the world-famous coastline, one of the most beautiful and serene in the UK; the Broads National Park, a magnet for thousands of visitors a year looking to enjoy the unique wetlands spread over Norfolk and Suffolk; a multitude of rivers including the wide slow Great Ouse and Nene in Cambridgeshire and the Yare, Wensum and Bure in Norfolk, and in Suffolk the River Stour in the inspirational Dedham Vale, famously known as Constables Country sits on the border with Essex.

Cambridgeshire itself is a vast flatland whose huge skies stretch from horizon to horizon, with roads and rivers criss-crossing the landscape and only ancient church spires spotted across the skyline. Norfolk has a magnificent coastline, quaint villages and a large forest, which it shares with Suffolk, whose equally beautiful coast is a must for anyone visiting the county, while not forgetting to visit its collection of old rustic villages with some of the best-preserved architecture from past times. It's hard to believe this is all only a short journey from the sprawling metropolis of London, and an easy day trip for anyone wishing to experience the quiet life. A rewarding and enriching time can be had in East Anglia.

This book is a collection of images from Norfolk, Suffolk and Cambridgeshire. I've travelled the length and breadth of this most wonderful area and brought you a selection of images to enjoy and hopefully persuade you to visit and experience for yourself what East Anglia has to offer.

NORFOLK

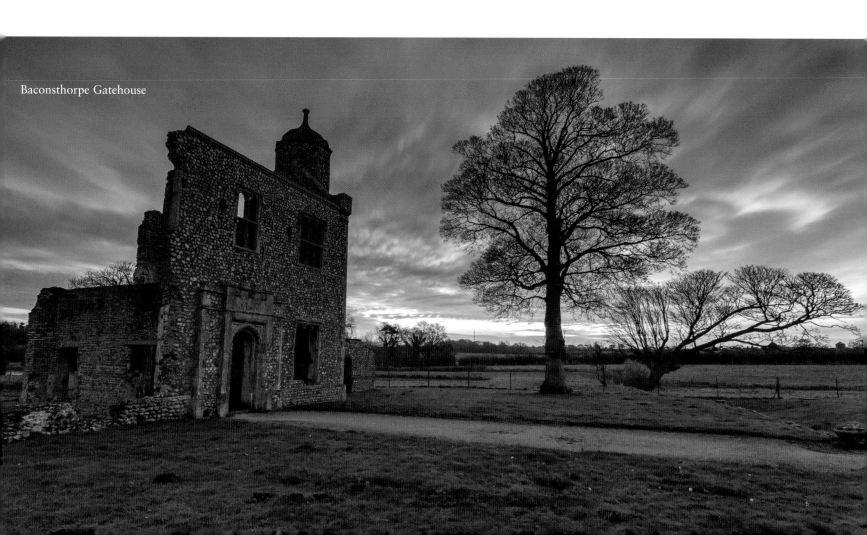

Baconsthorpe Gatehouse

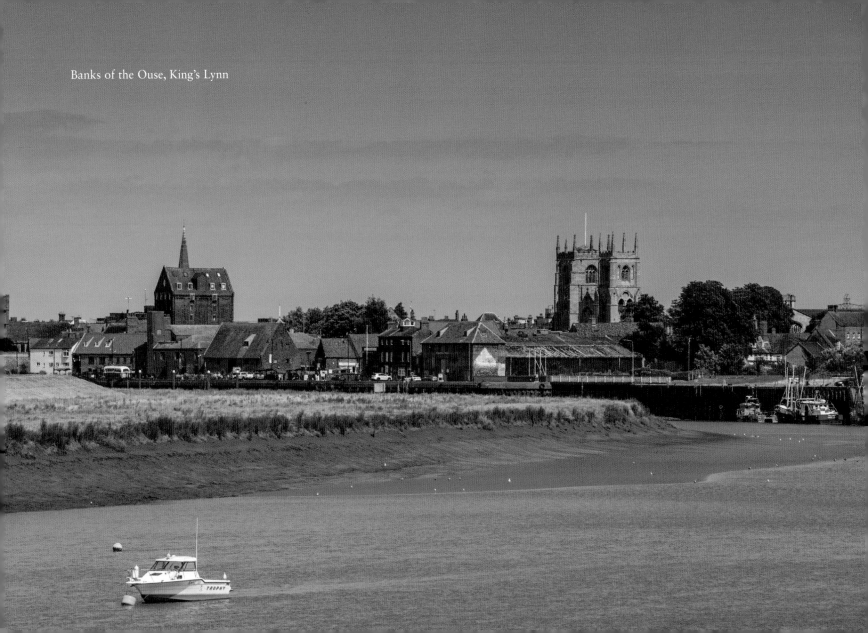

Banks of the Ouse, King's Lynn

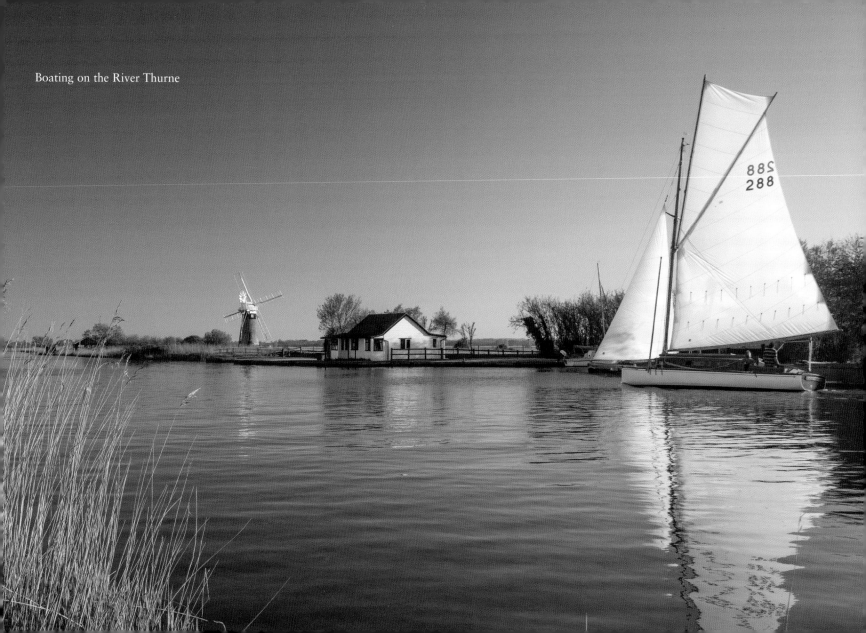

Boating on the River Thurne

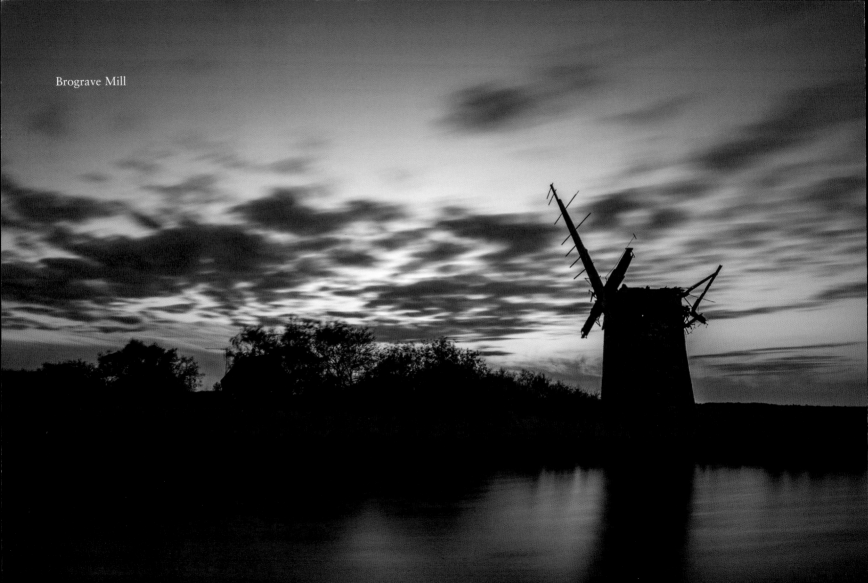

Brograve Mill

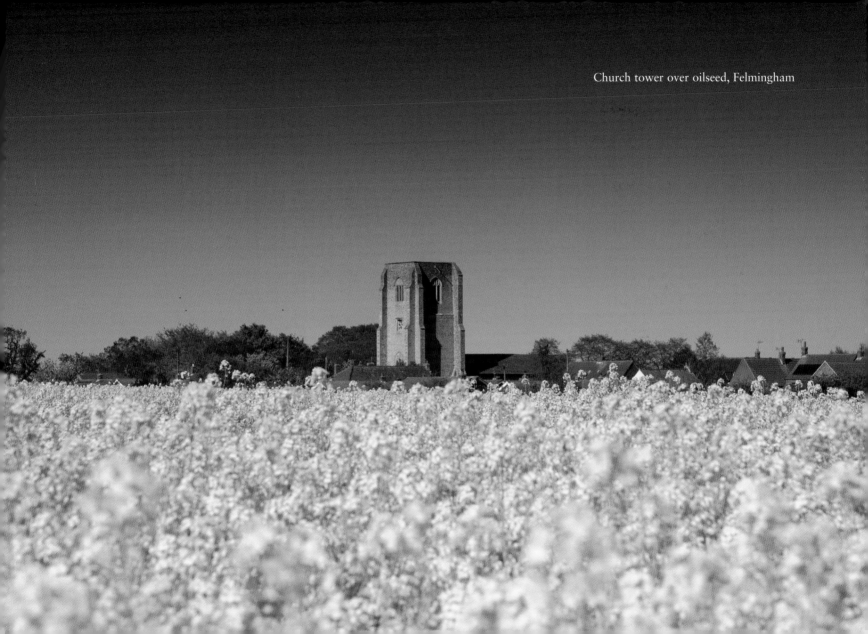

Church tower over oilseed, Felmingham

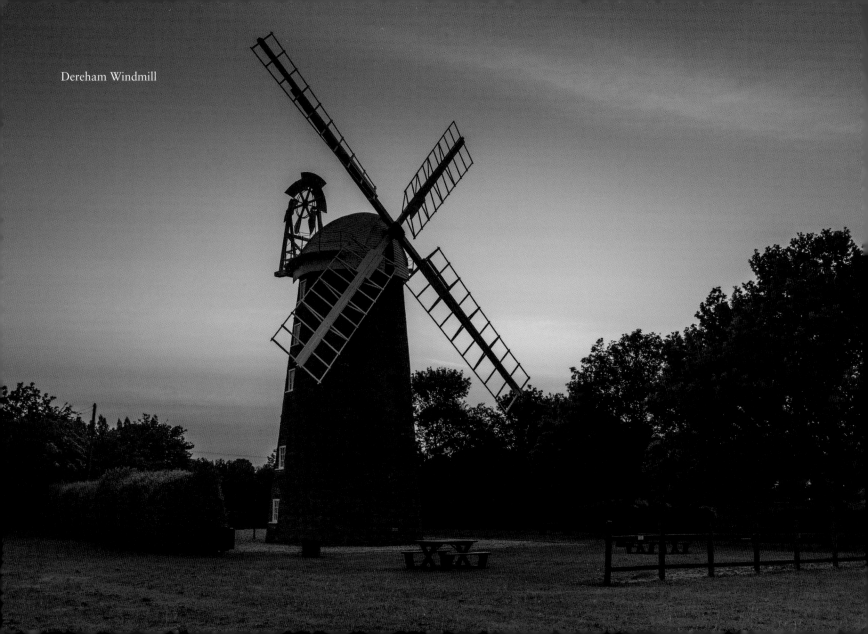

Dereham Windmill

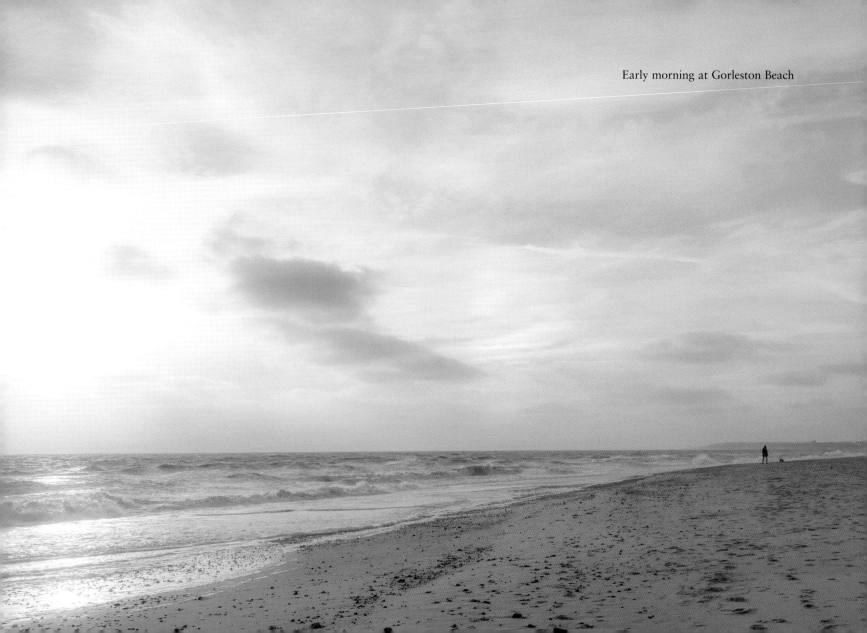

Early morning at Gorleston Beach

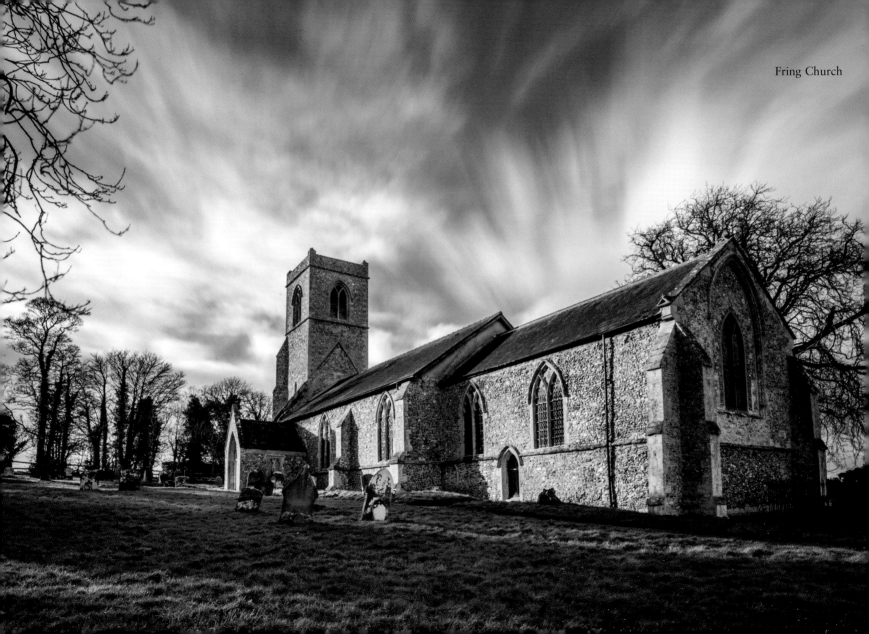

Fring Church

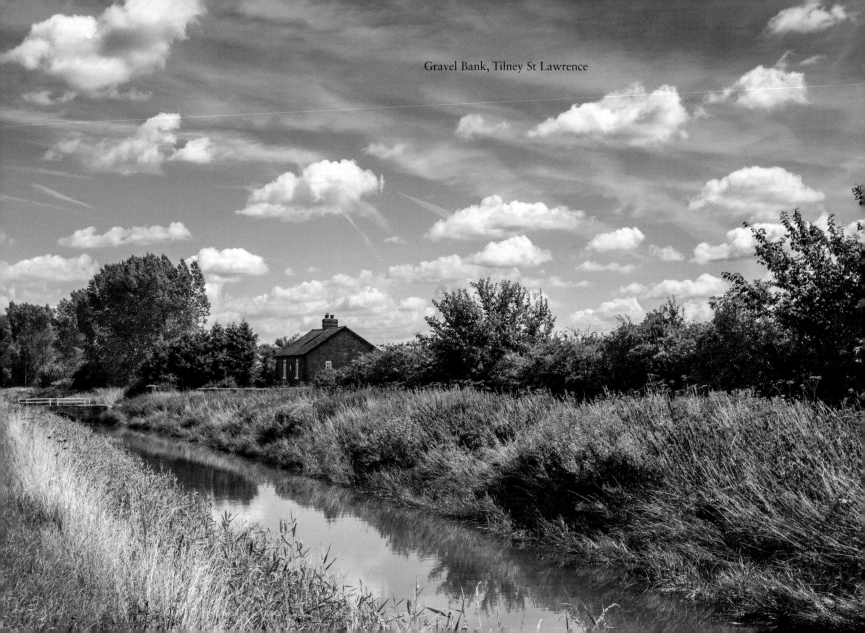

Gravel Bank, Tilney St Lawrence

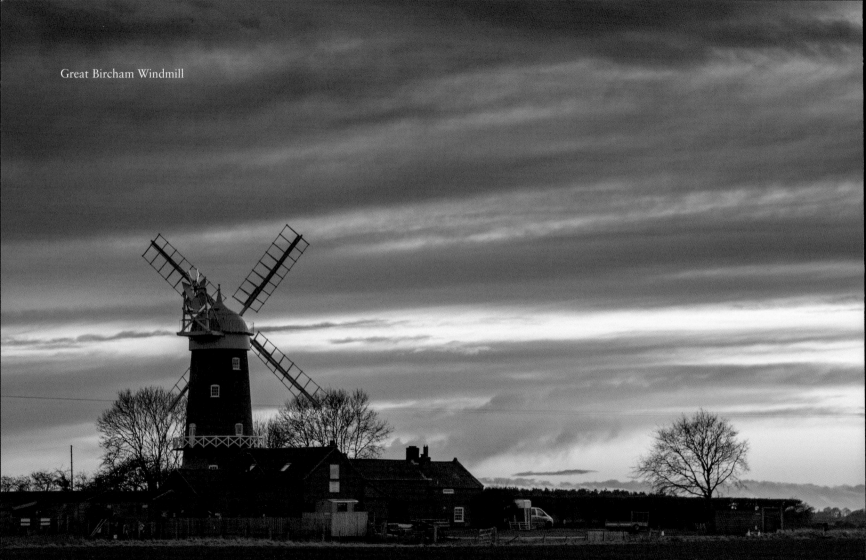

Great Bircham Windmill

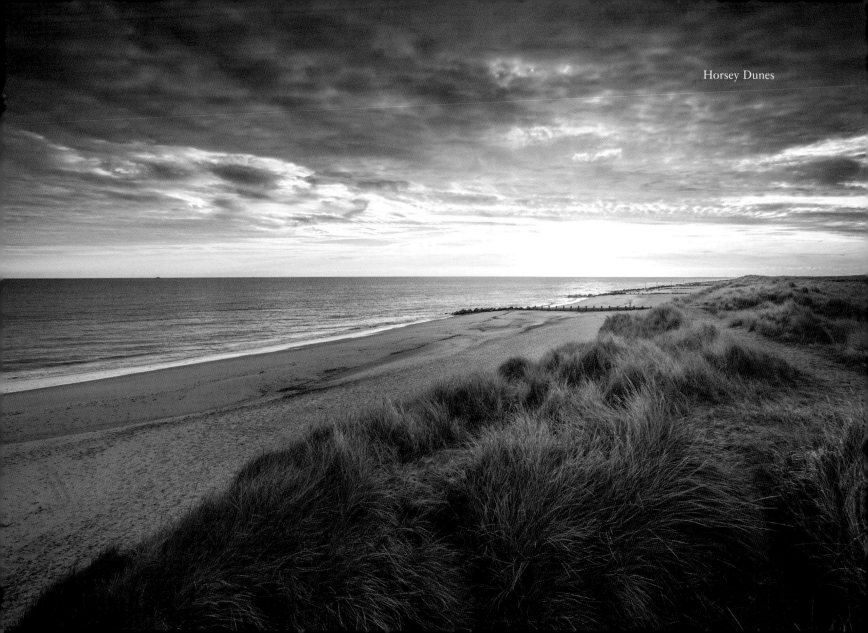

Horsey Dunes

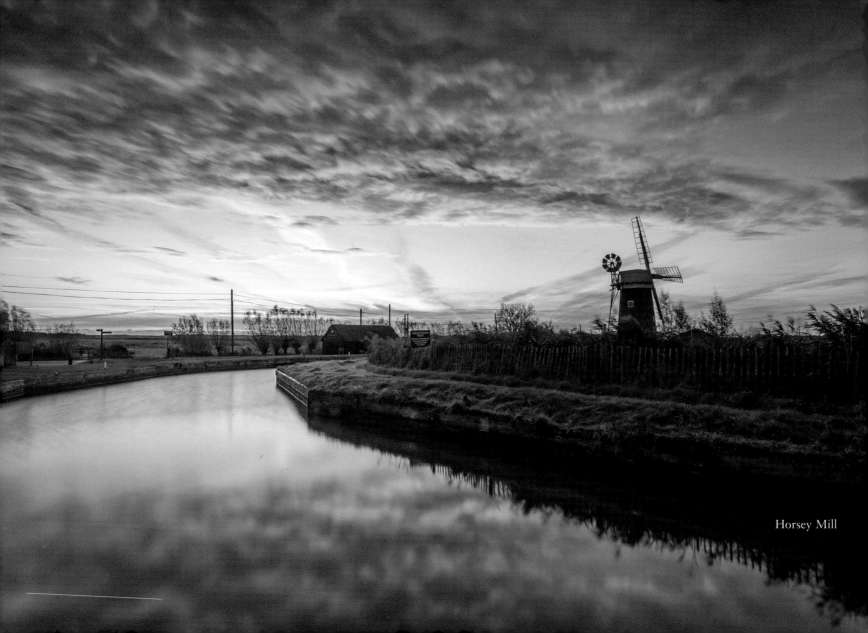

Horsey Mill

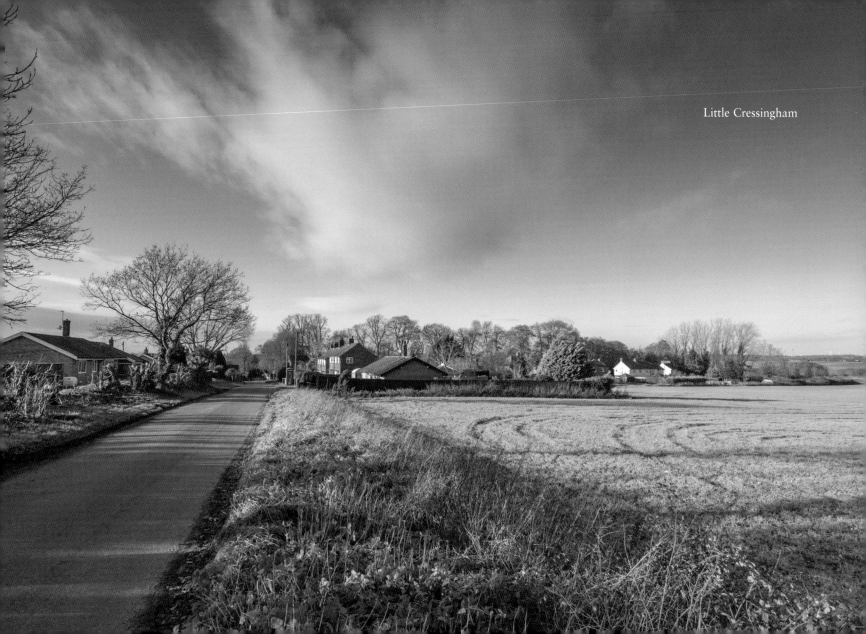

Little Cressingham

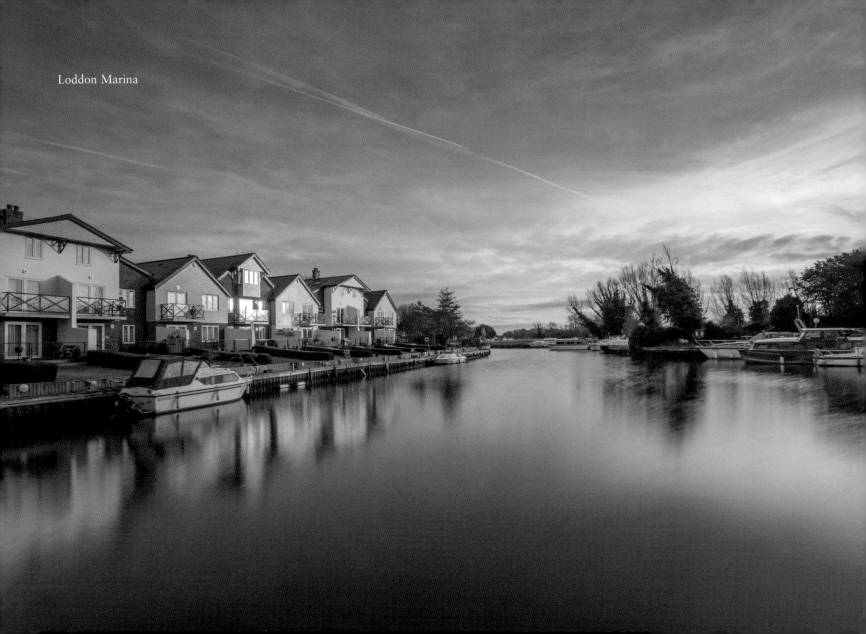

Loddon Marina

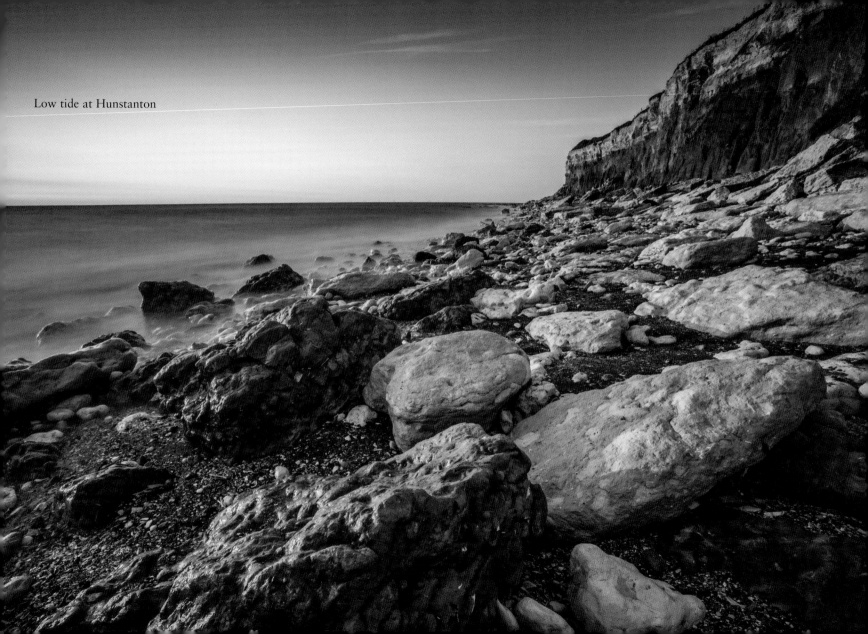

Low tide at Hunstanton

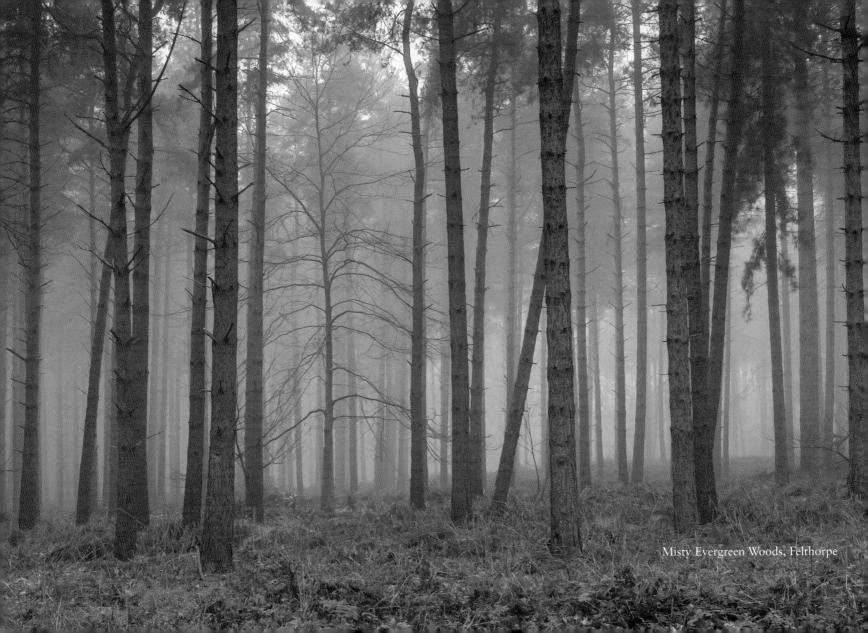

Misty Evergreen Woods, Felthorpe

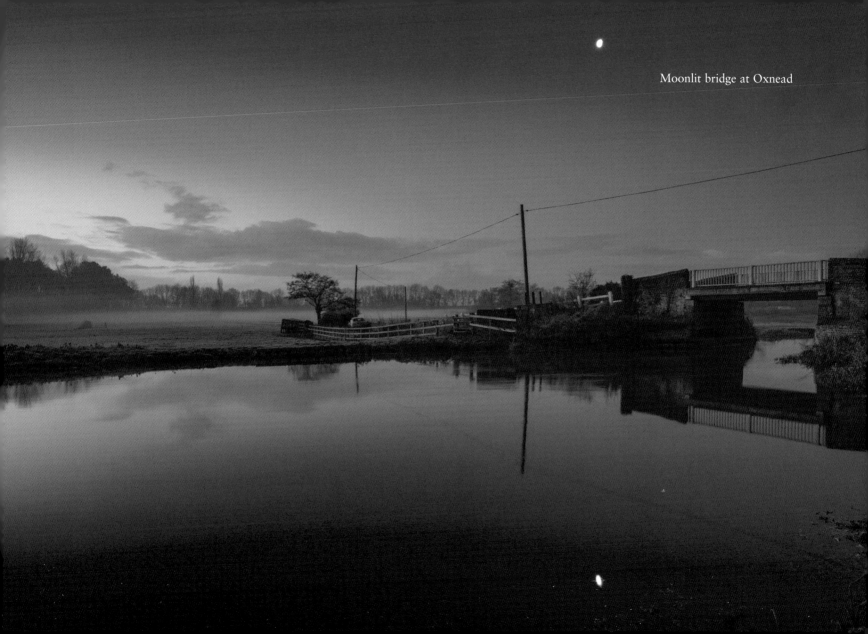

Moonlit bridge at Oxnead

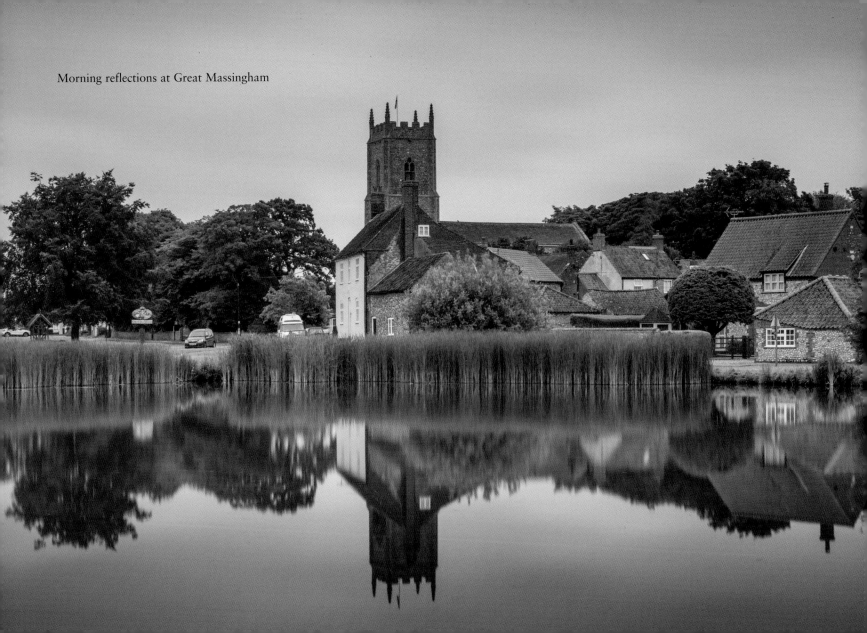

Morning reflections at Great Massingham

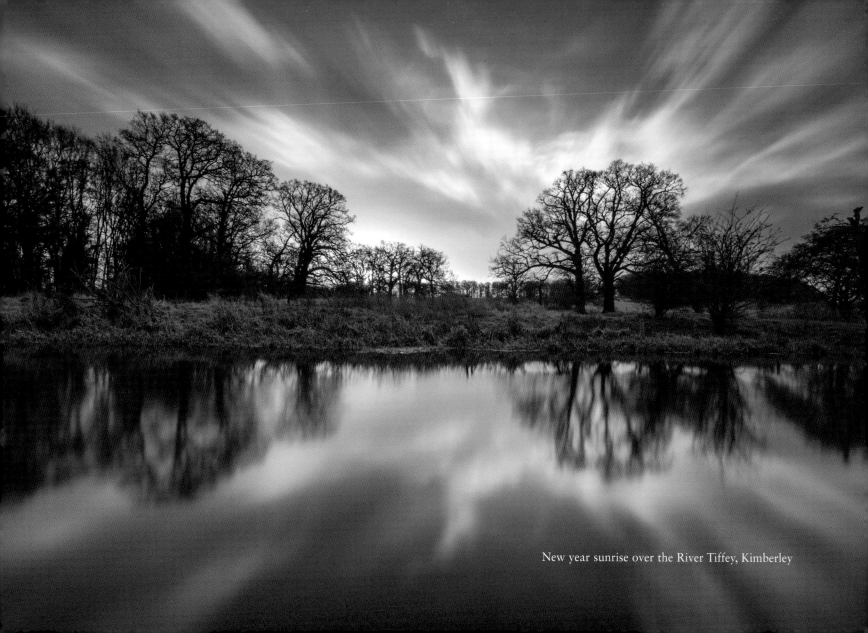

New year sunrise over the River Tiffey, Kimberley

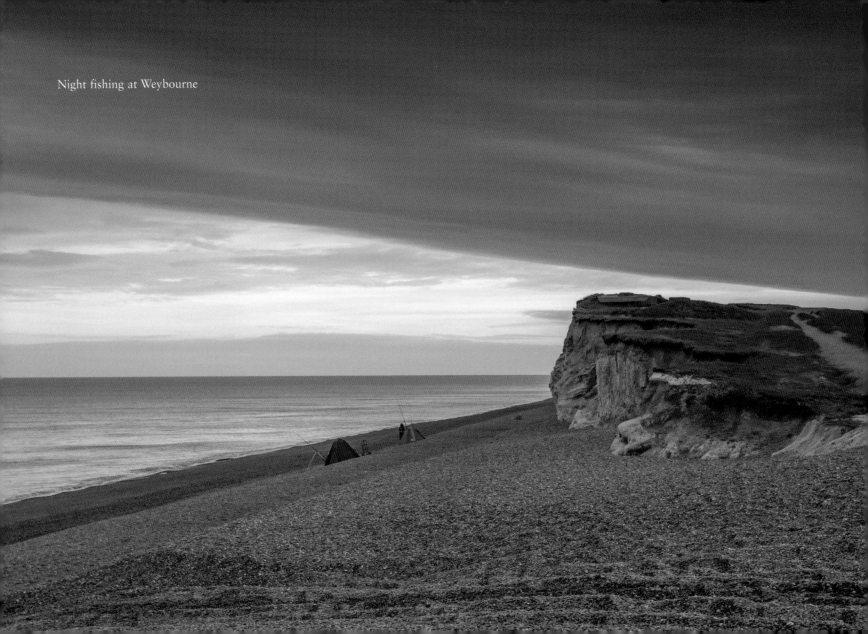

Night fishing at Weybourne

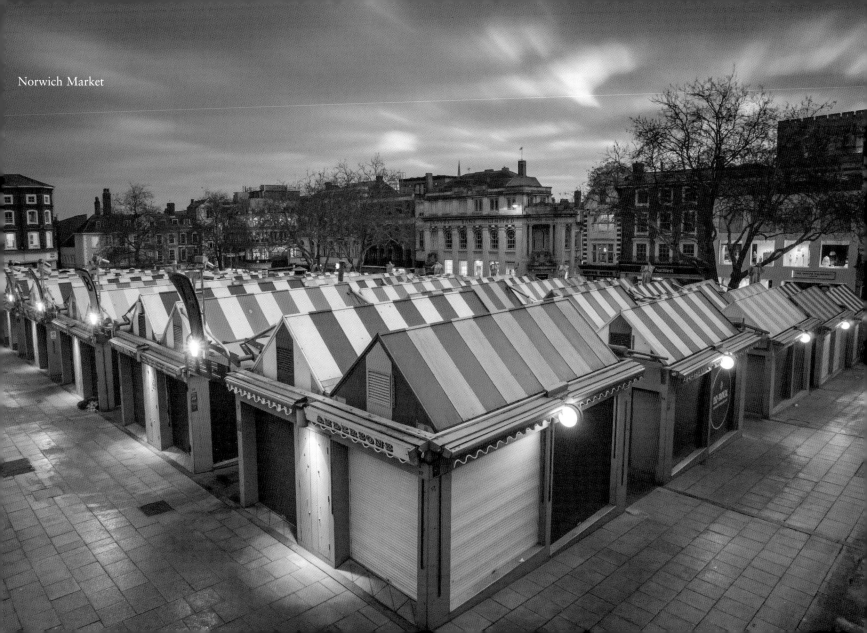

Norwich Market

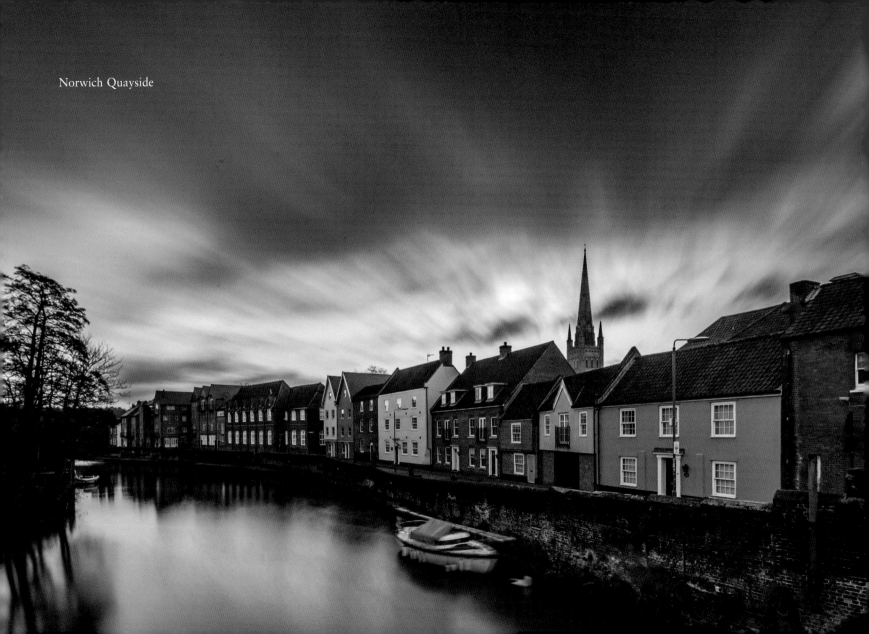

Norwich Quayside

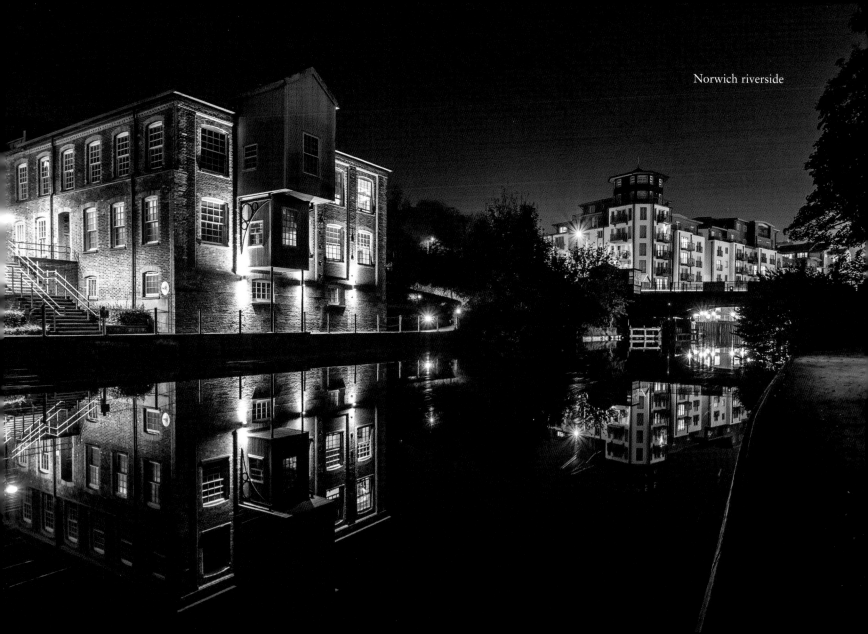

Norwich riverside

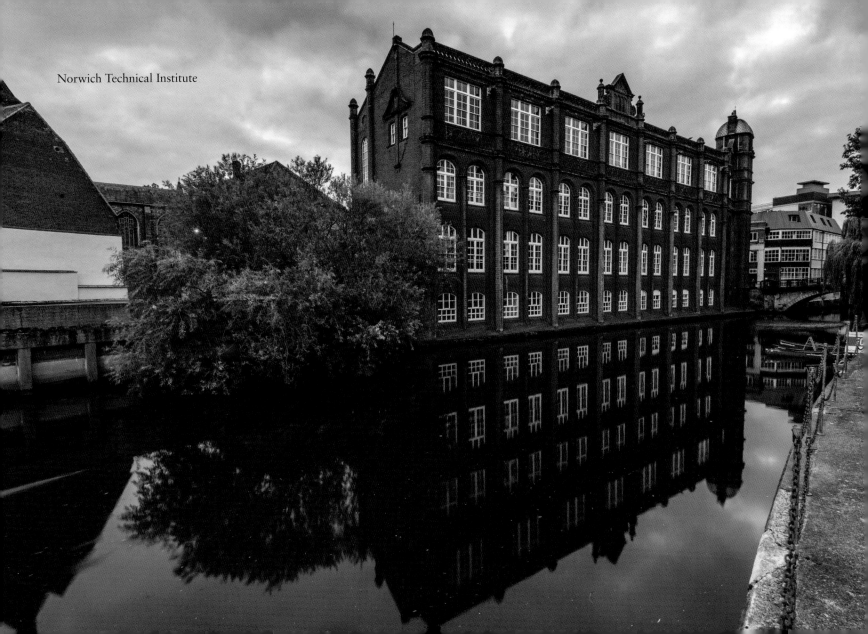

Norwich Technical Institute

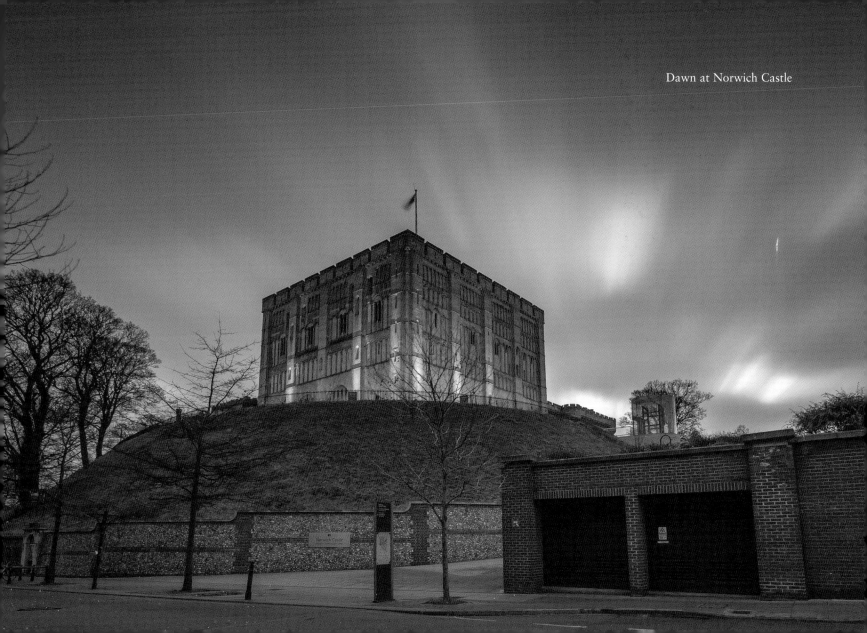
Dawn at Norwich Castle

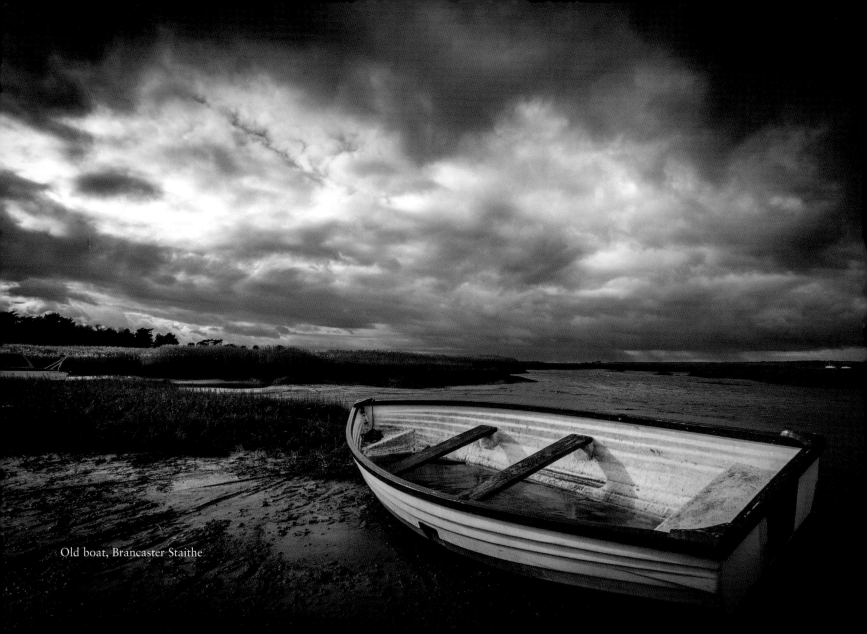
Old boat, Brancaster Staithe

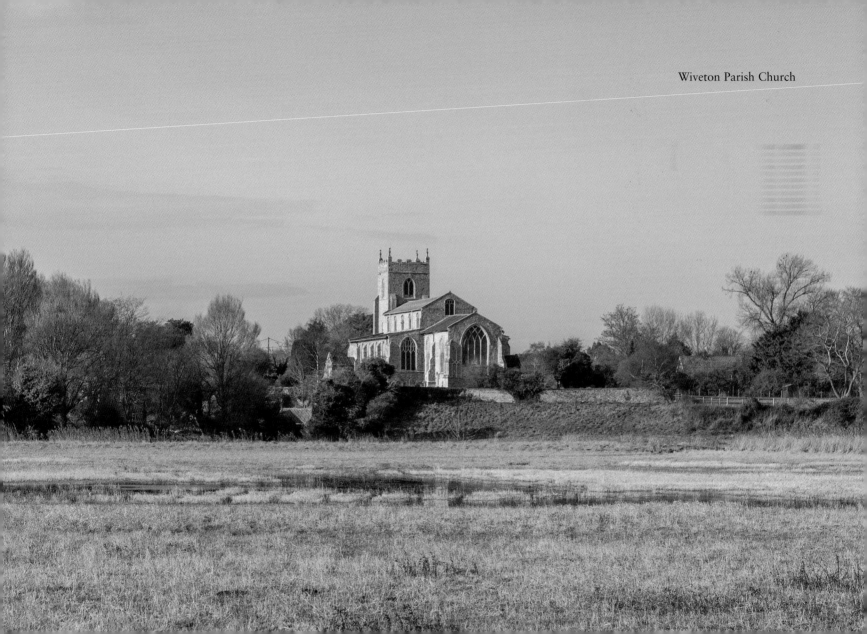

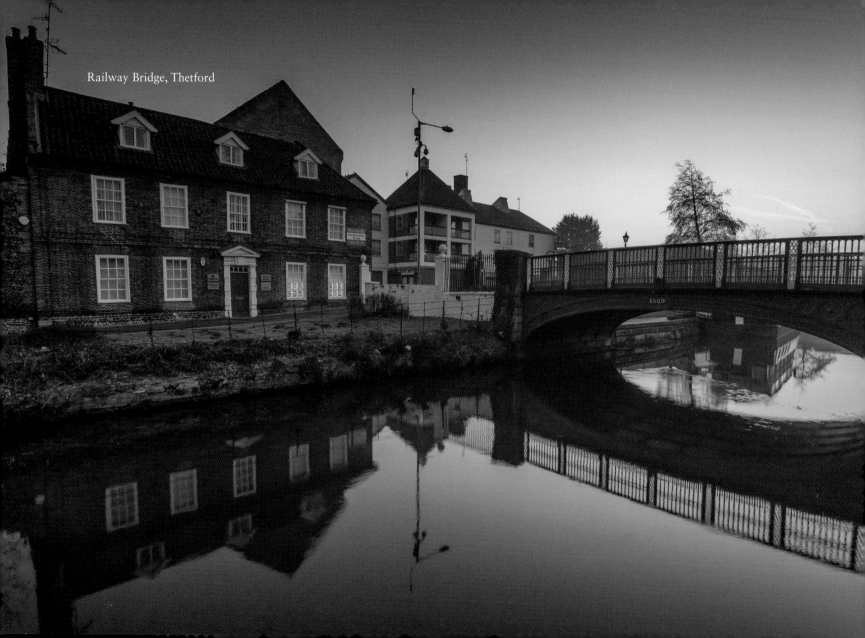

Railway Bridge, Thetford

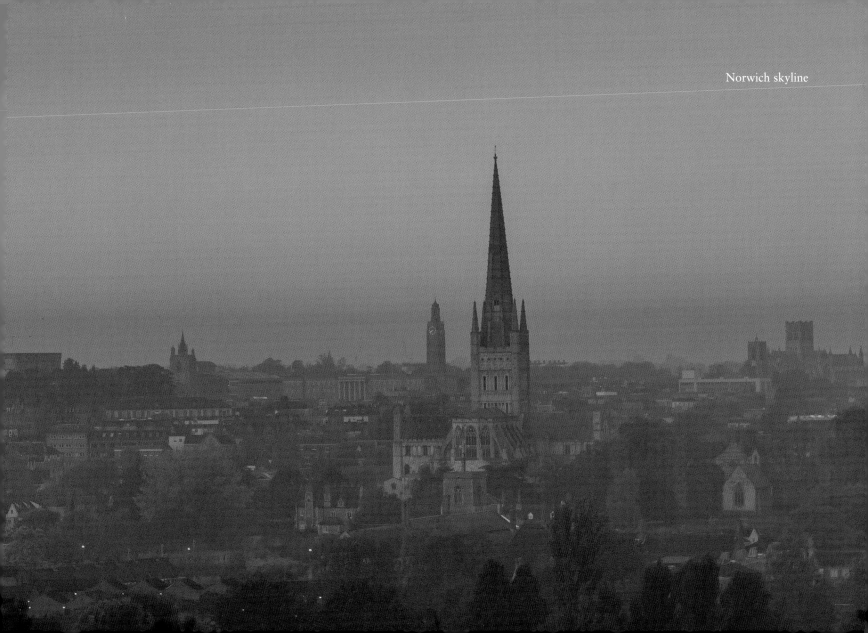

Norwich skyline

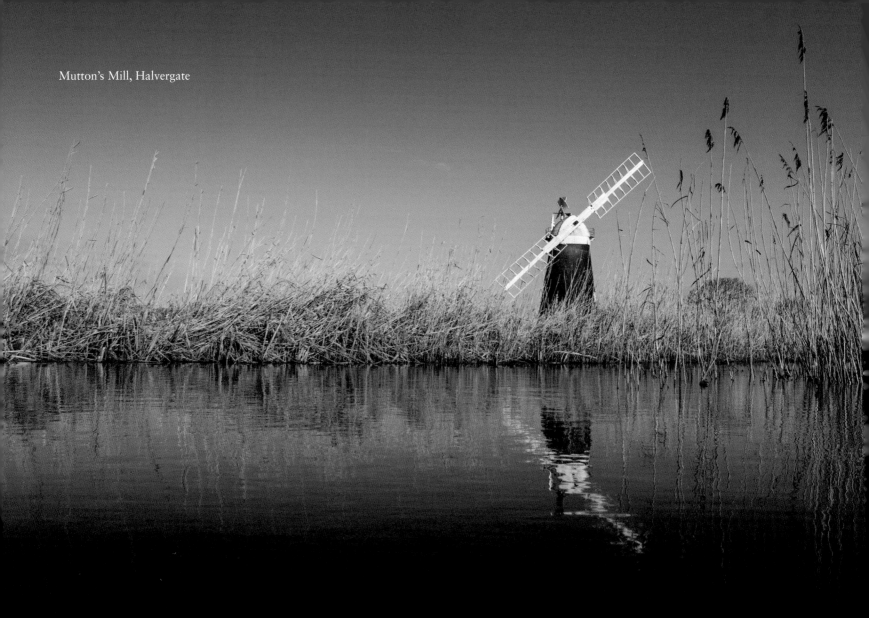

Mutton's Mill, Halvergate

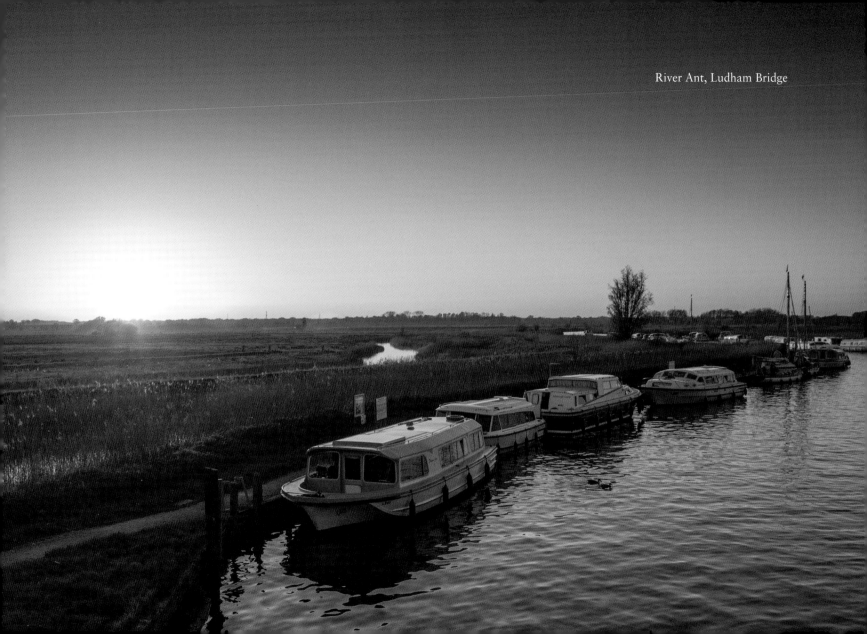

River Ant, Ludham Bridge

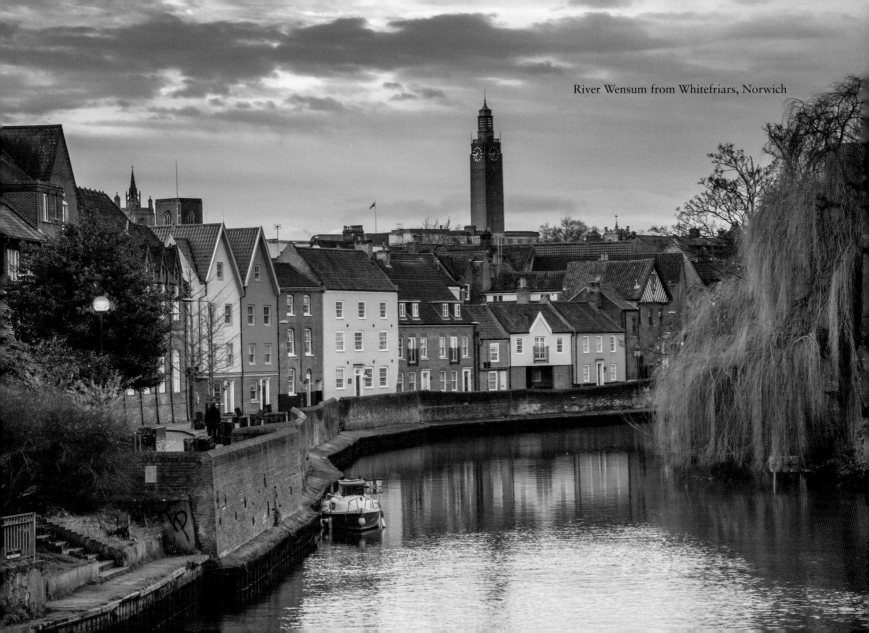

River Wensum from Whitefriars, Norwich

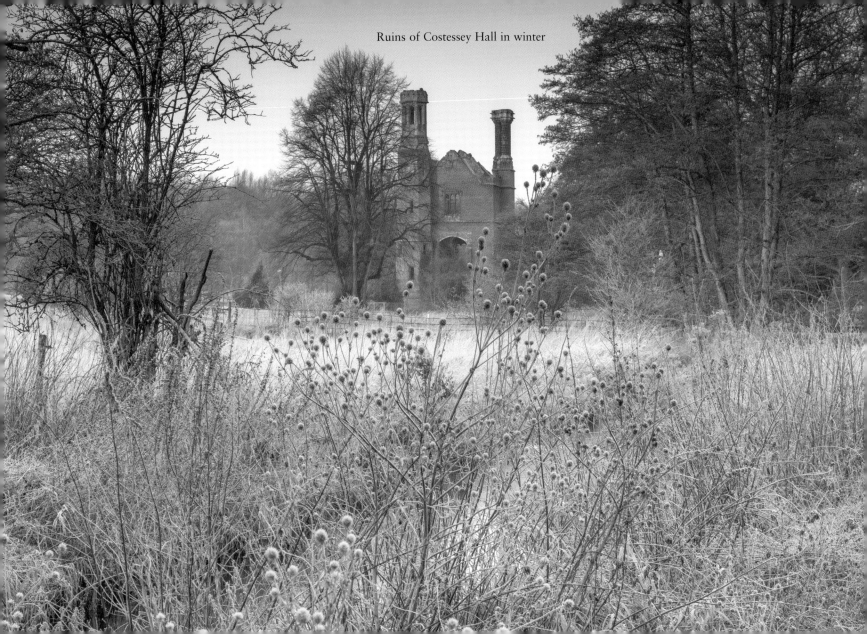

Ruins of Costessey Hall in winter

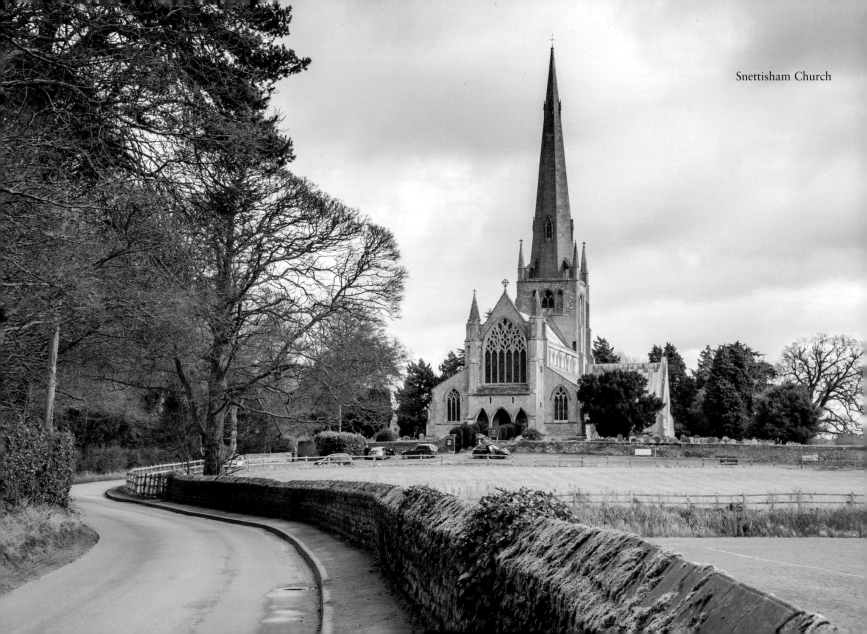

Snettisham Church

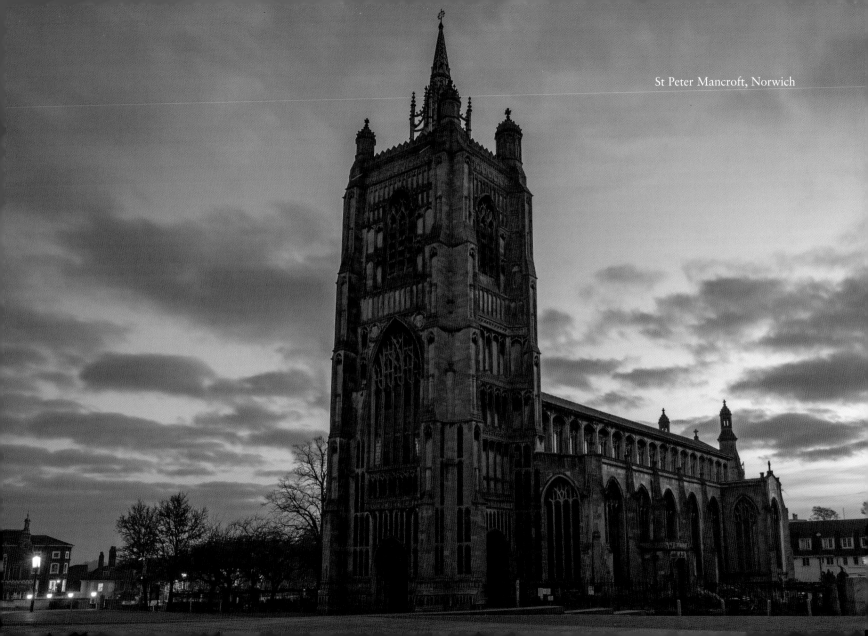

St Peter Mancroft, Norwich

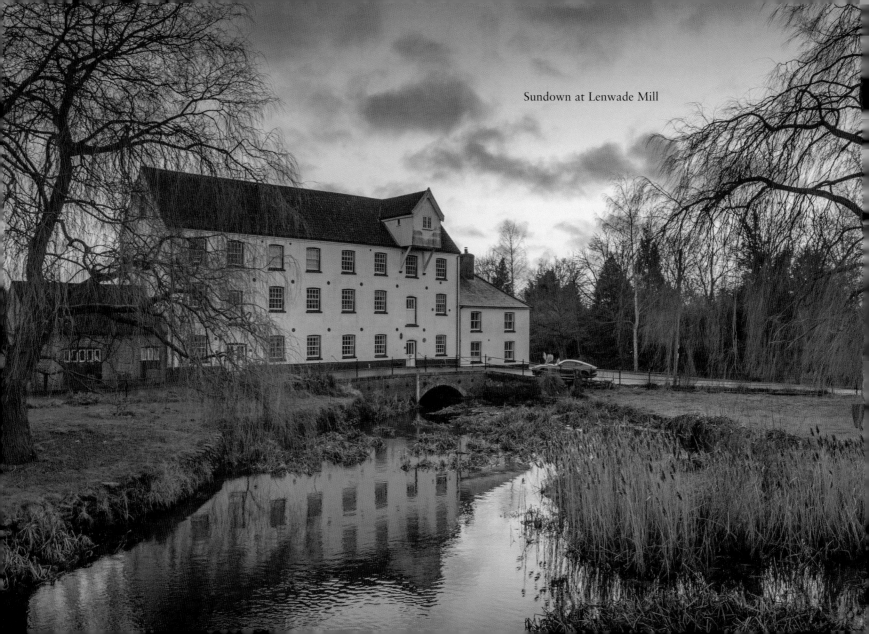

Sundown at Lenwade Mill

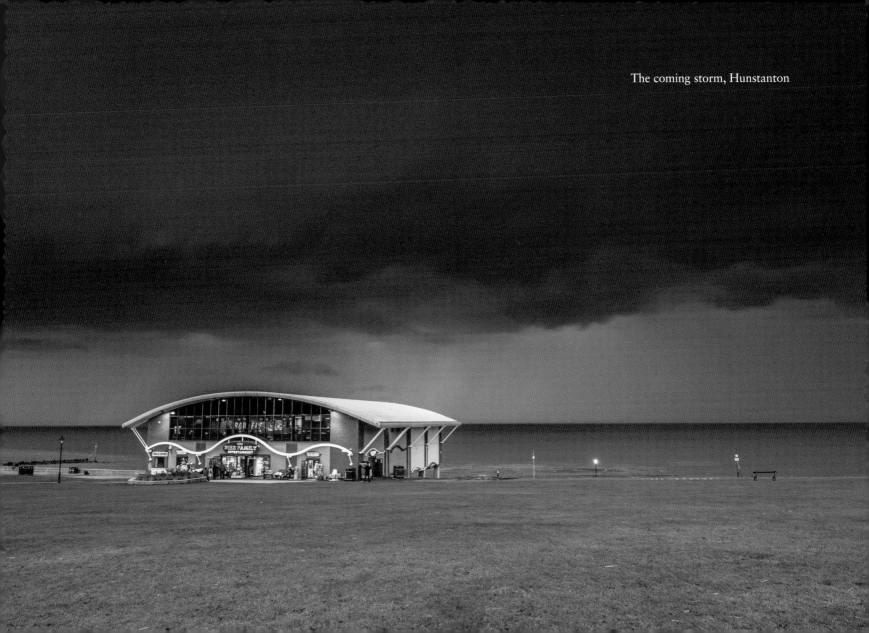

The coming storm, Hunstanton

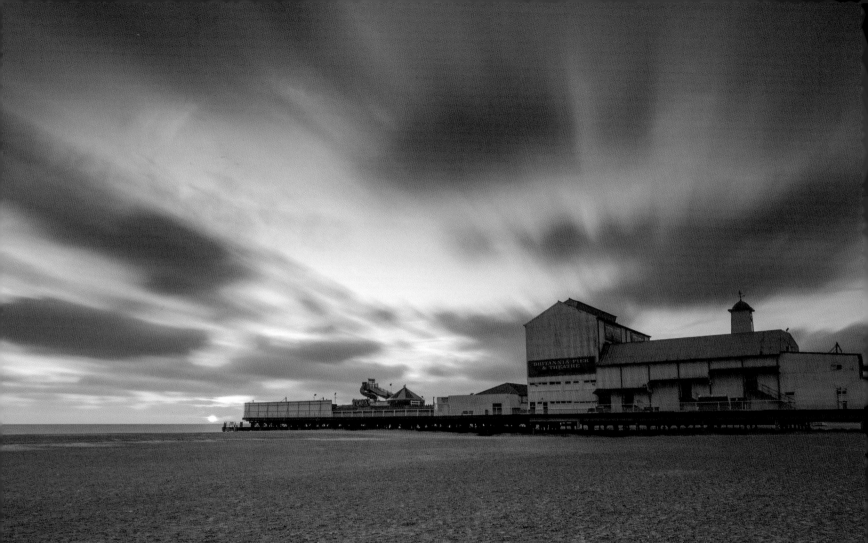

The pier at Great Yarmouth

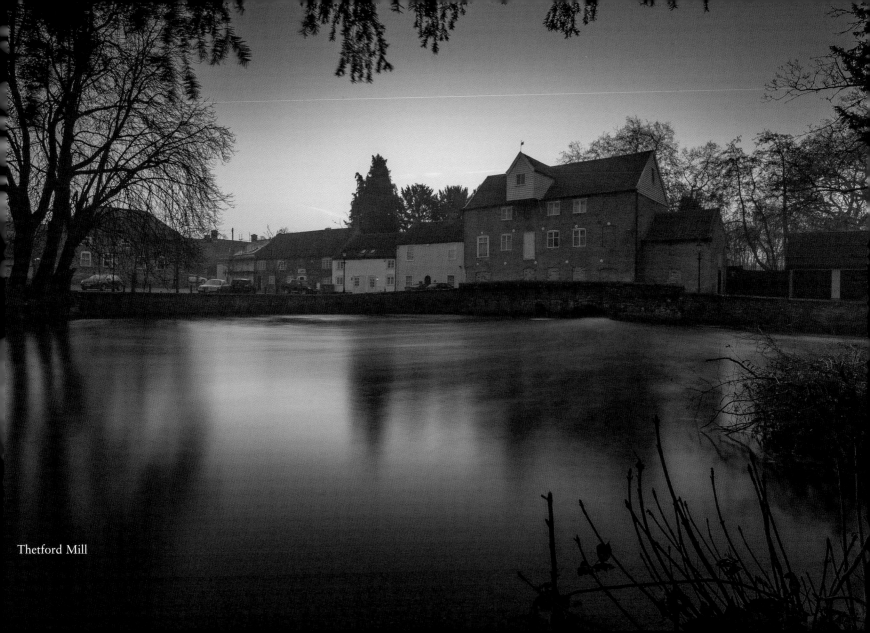

Thetford Mill

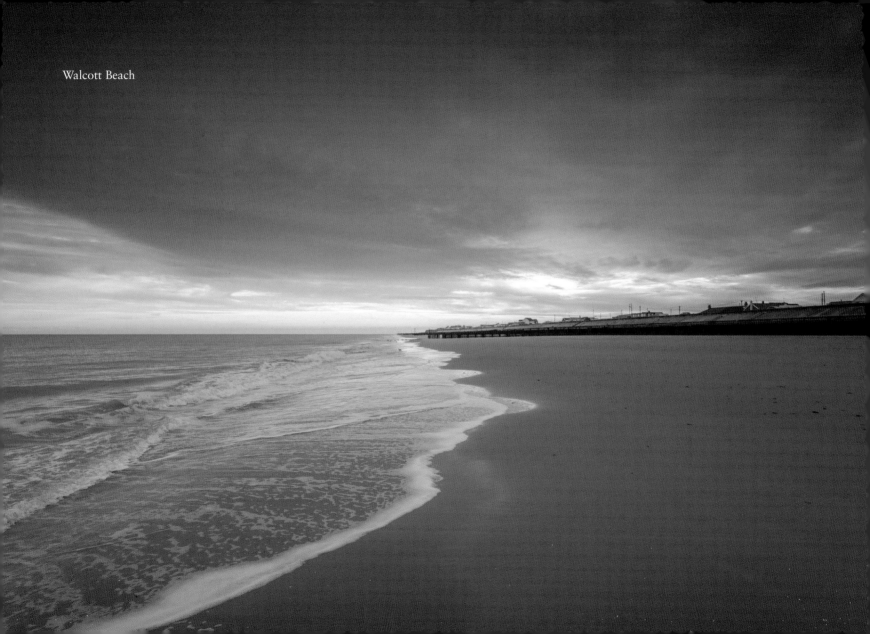

Walcott Beach

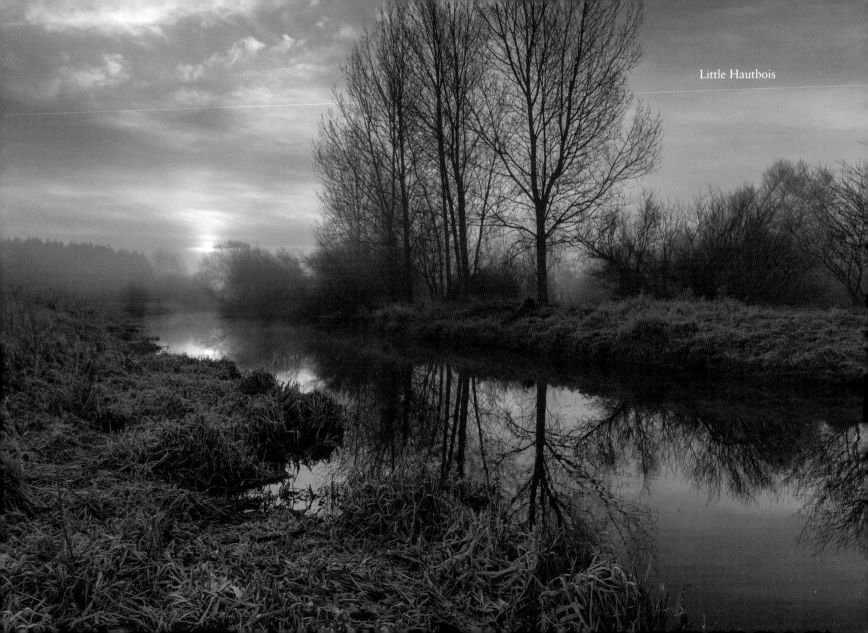

Little Hautbois

SUFFOLK

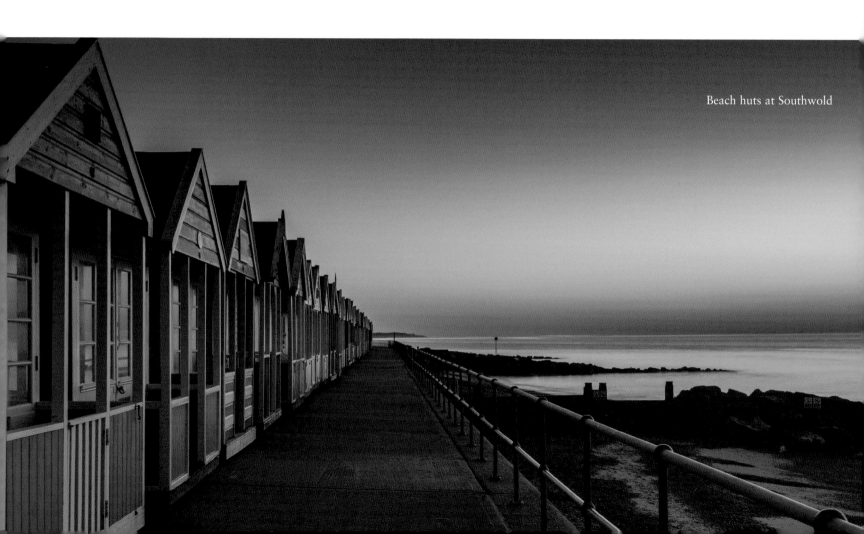

Beach huts at Southwold

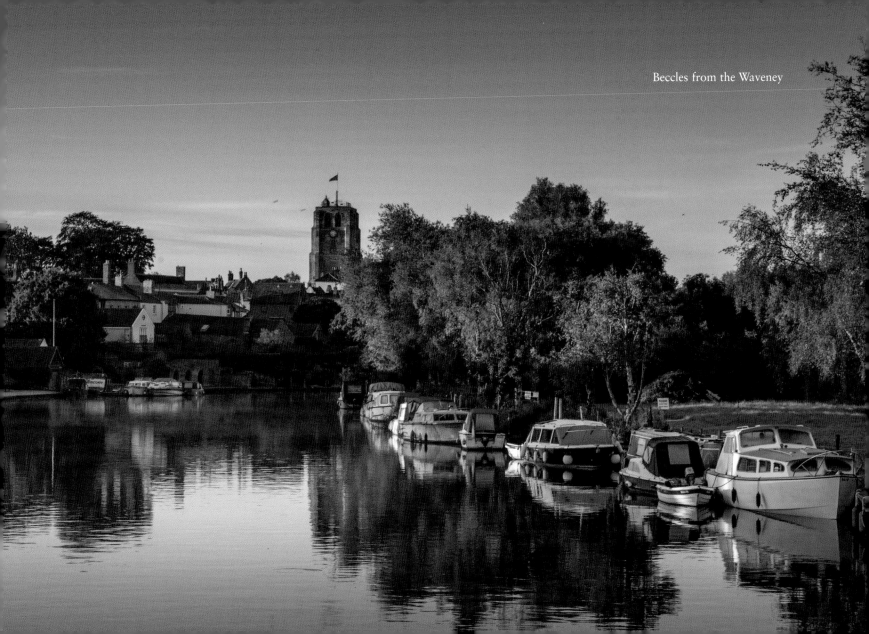

Beccles from the Waveney

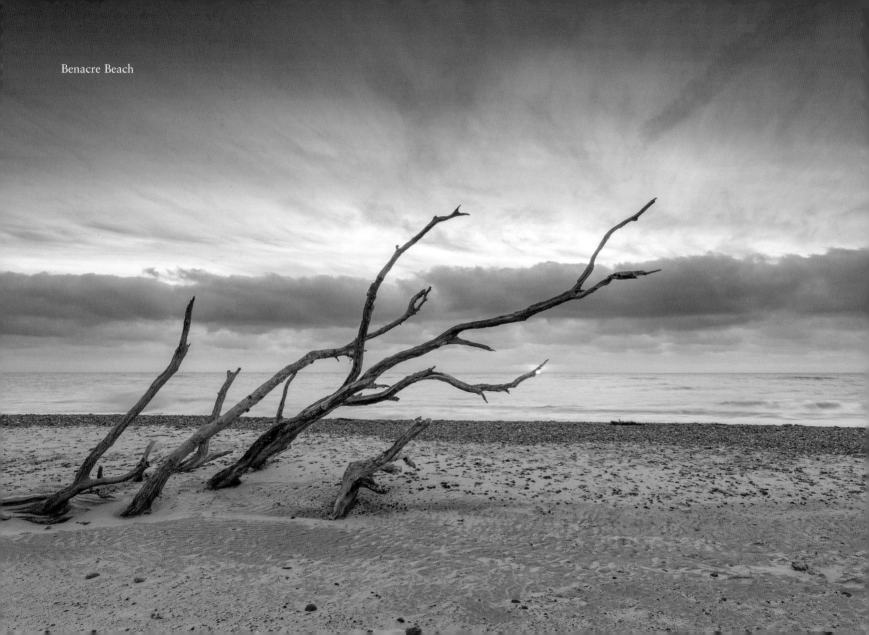

Benacre Beach

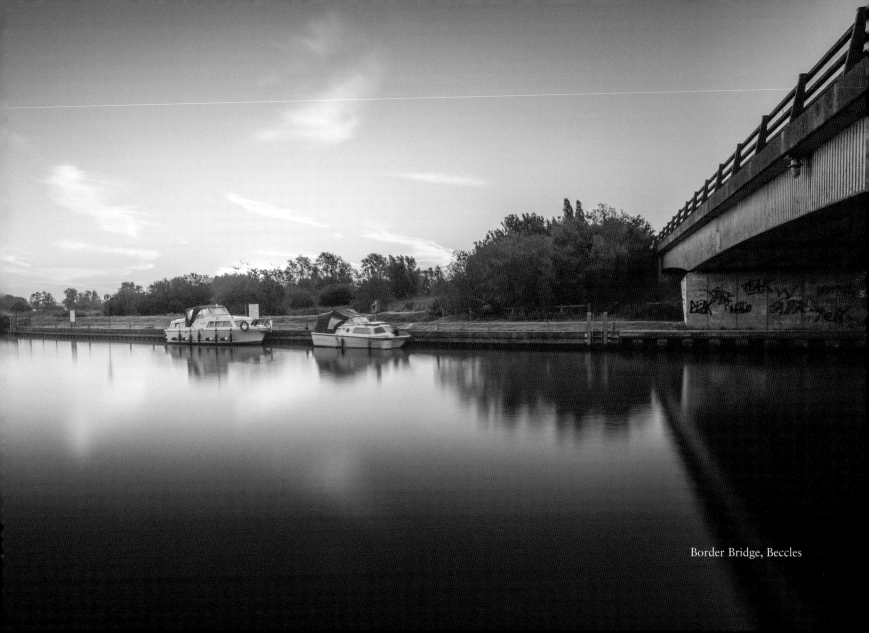

Border Bridge, Beccles

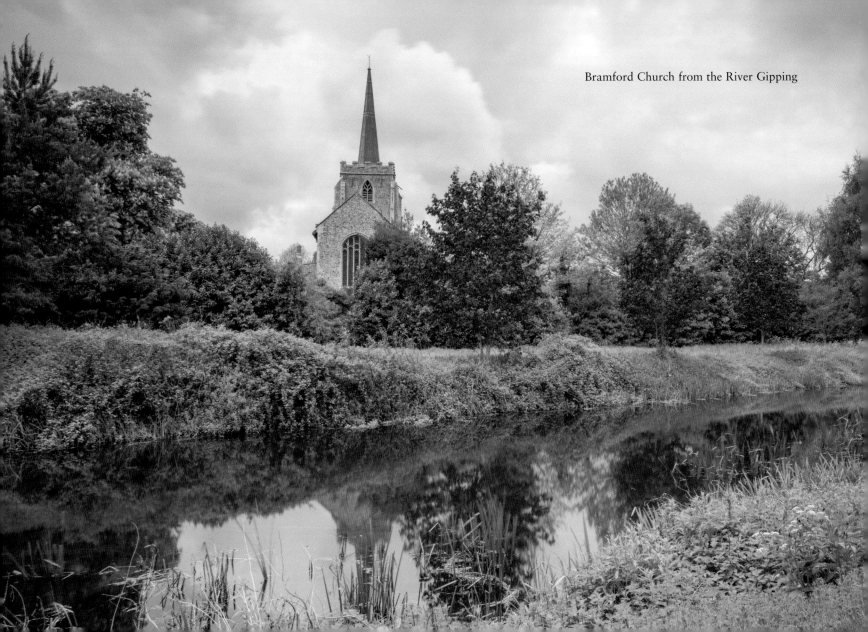

Bramford Church from the River Gipping

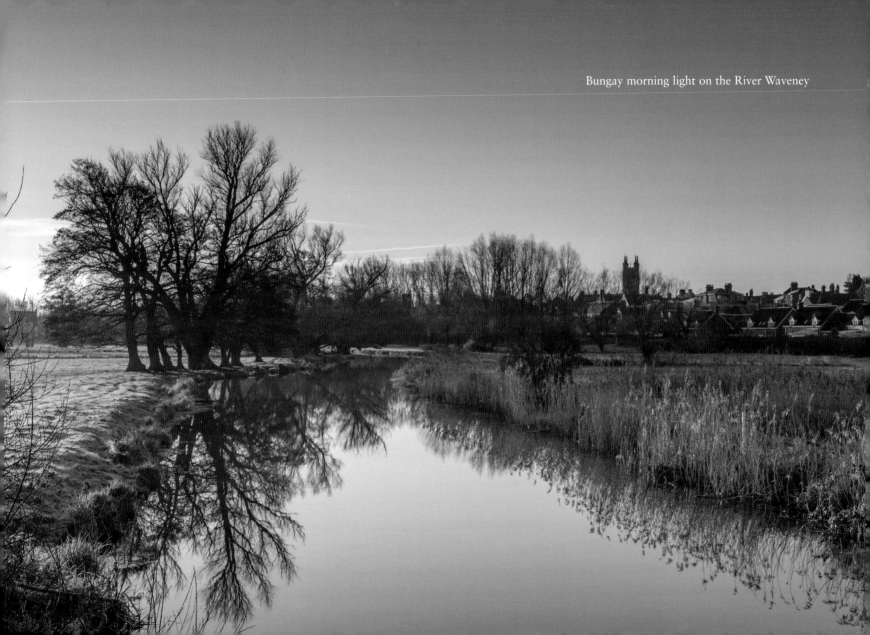

Bungay morning light on the River Waveney

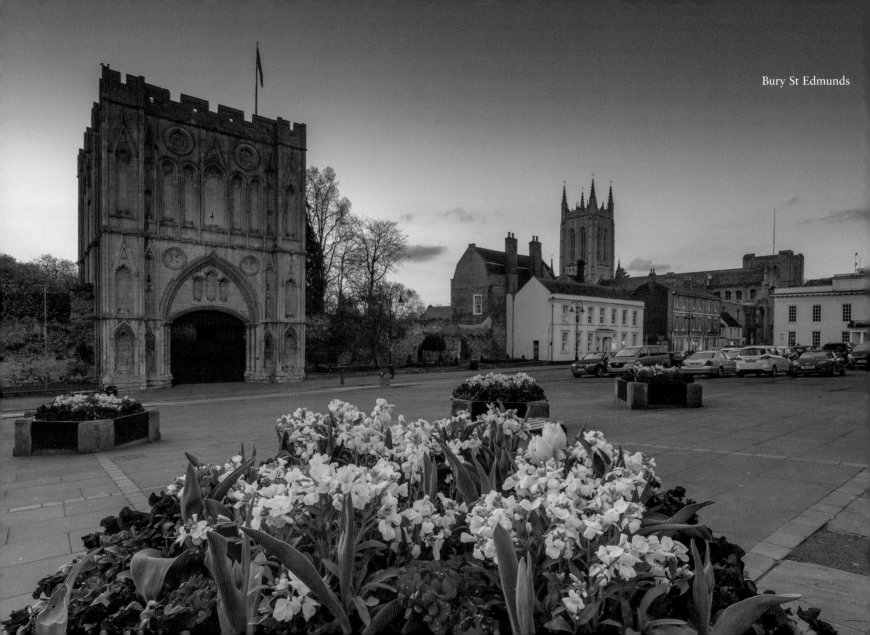

Bury St Edmunds

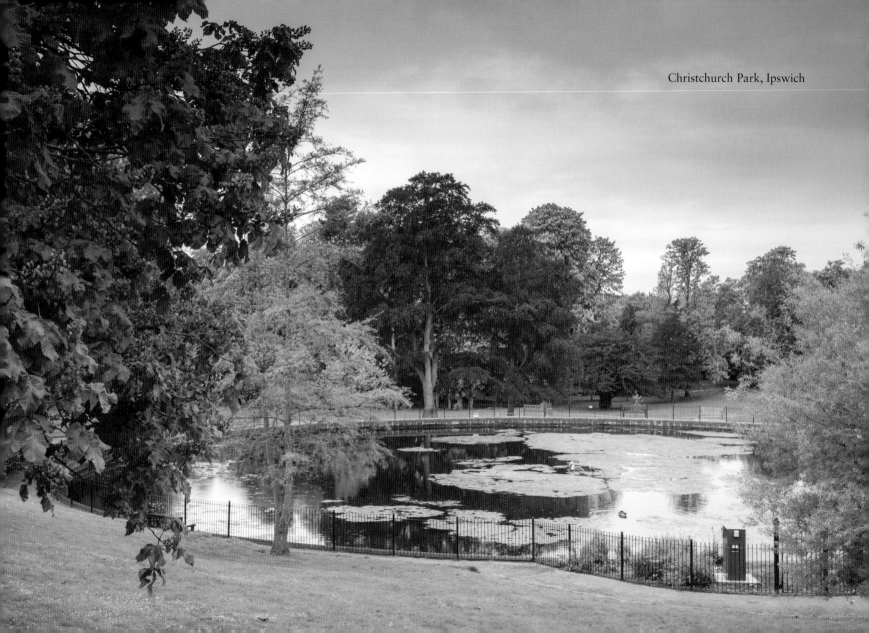

Christchurch Park, Ipswich

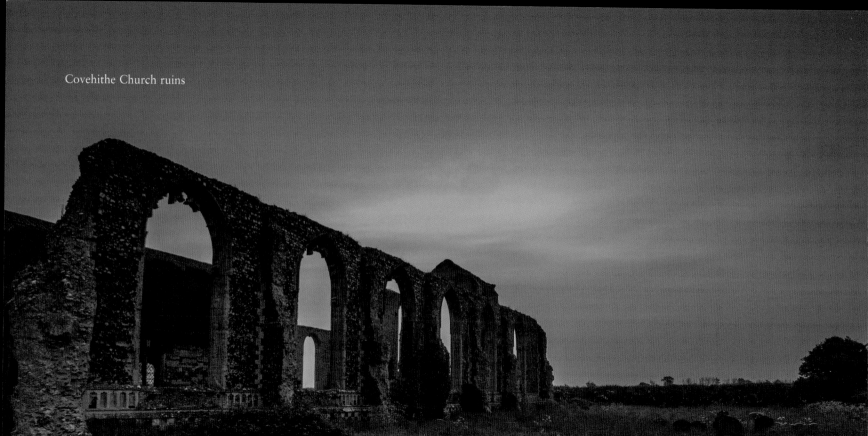

Covehithe Church ruins

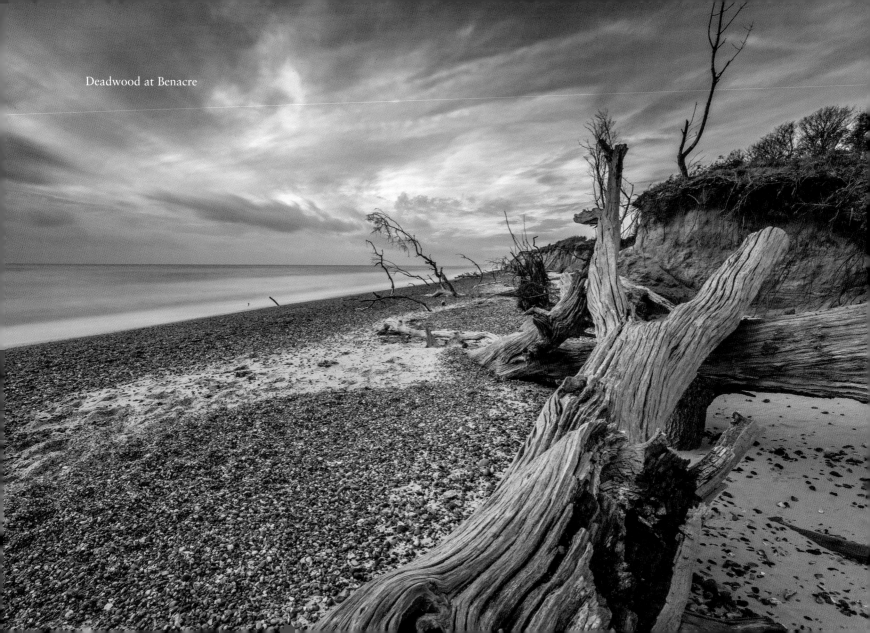

Deadwood at Benacre

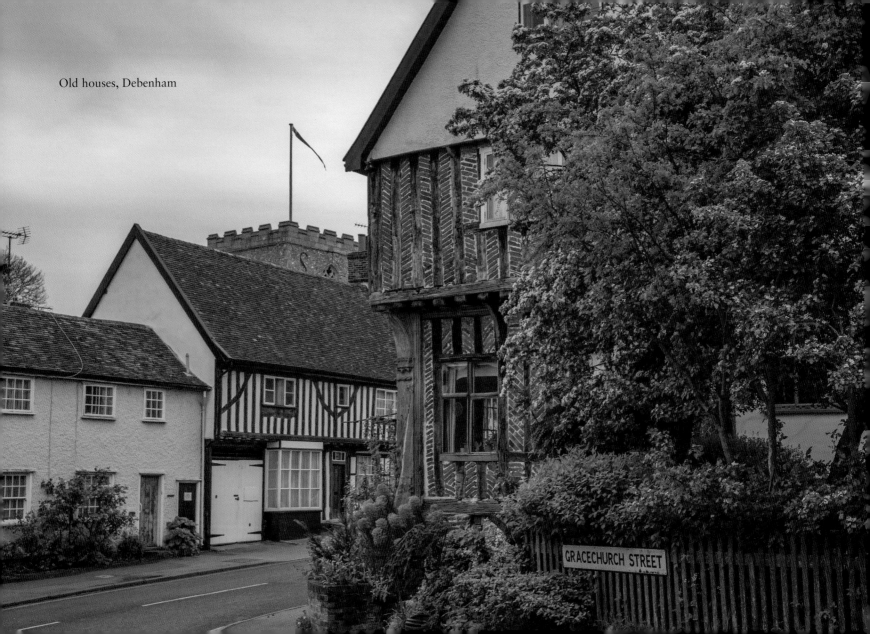

Old houses, Debenham

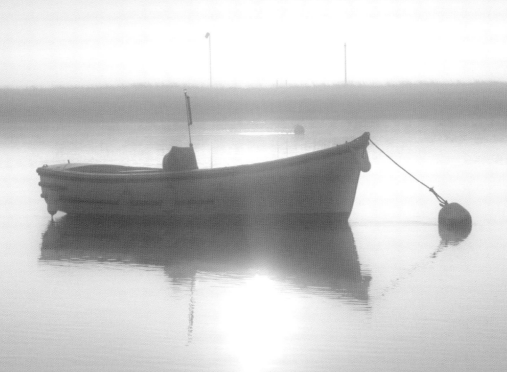

The dreamlike River Alde, Orford Ness

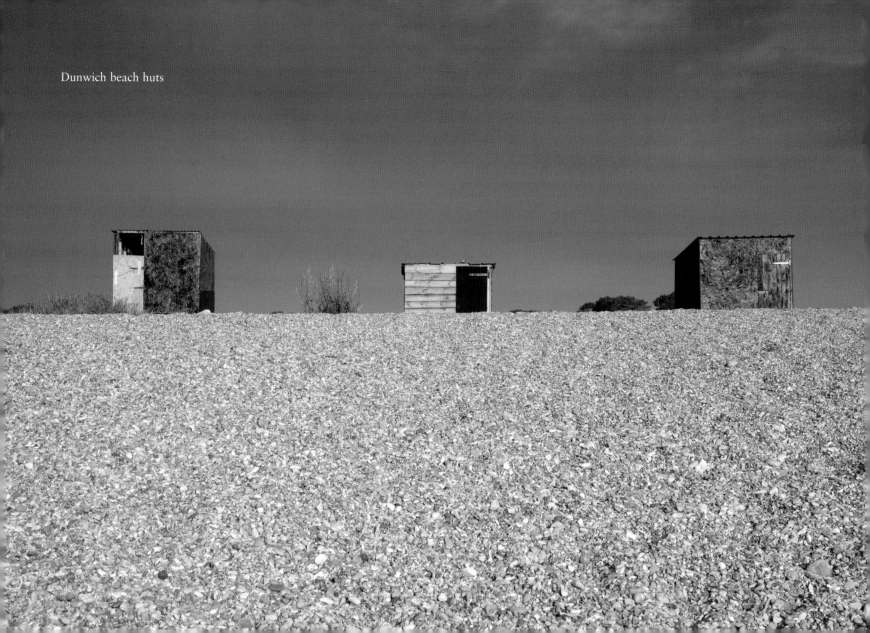

Dunwich beach huts

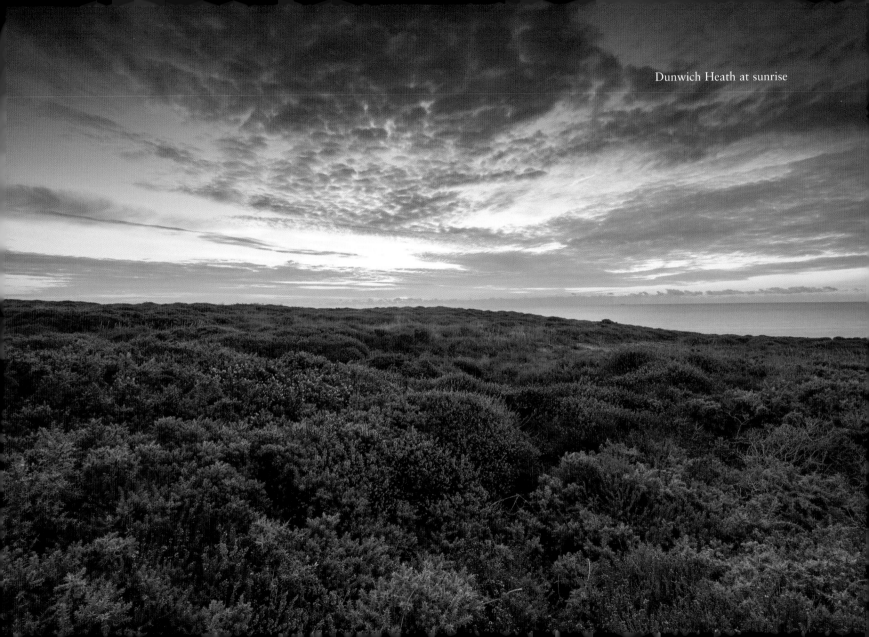

Dunwich Heath at sunrise

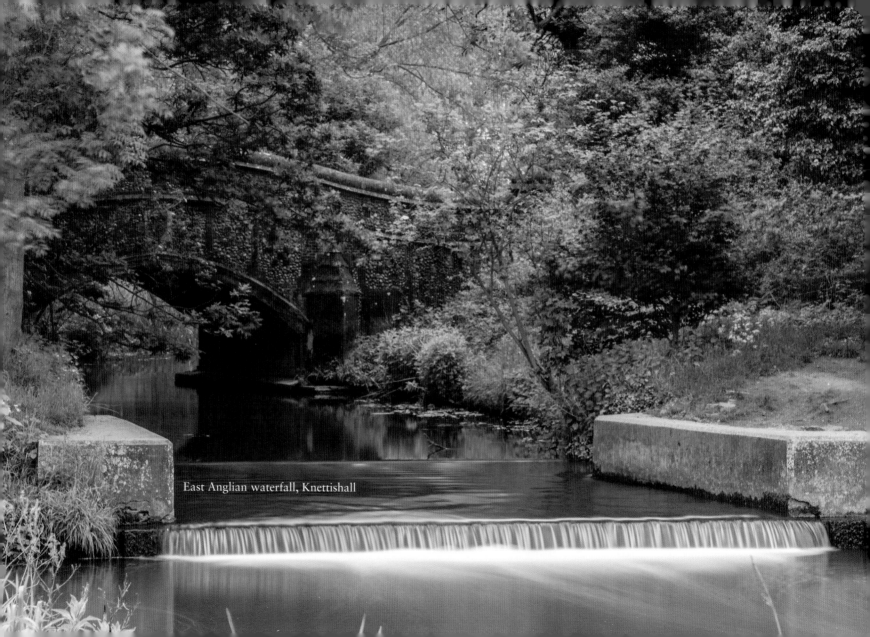

East Anglian waterfall, Knettishall

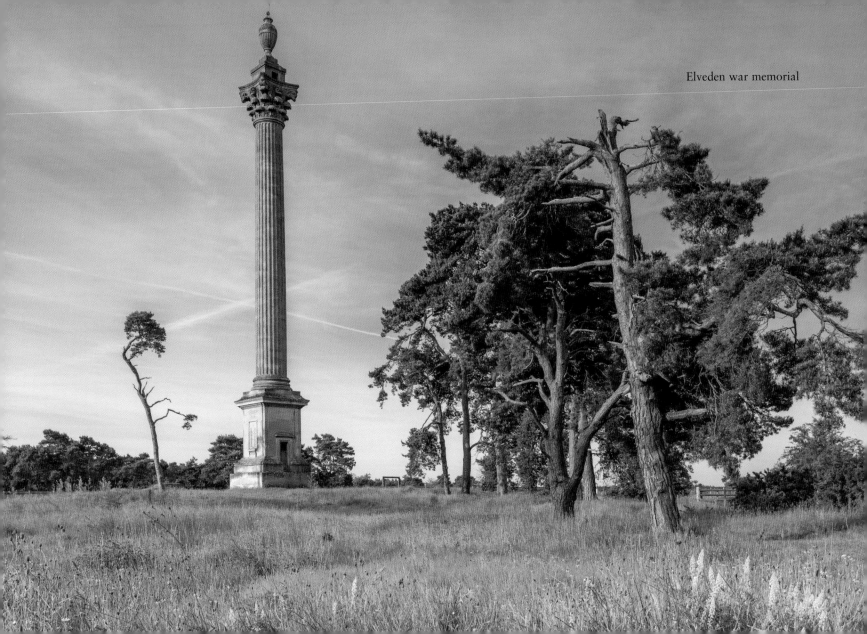

Elveden war memorial

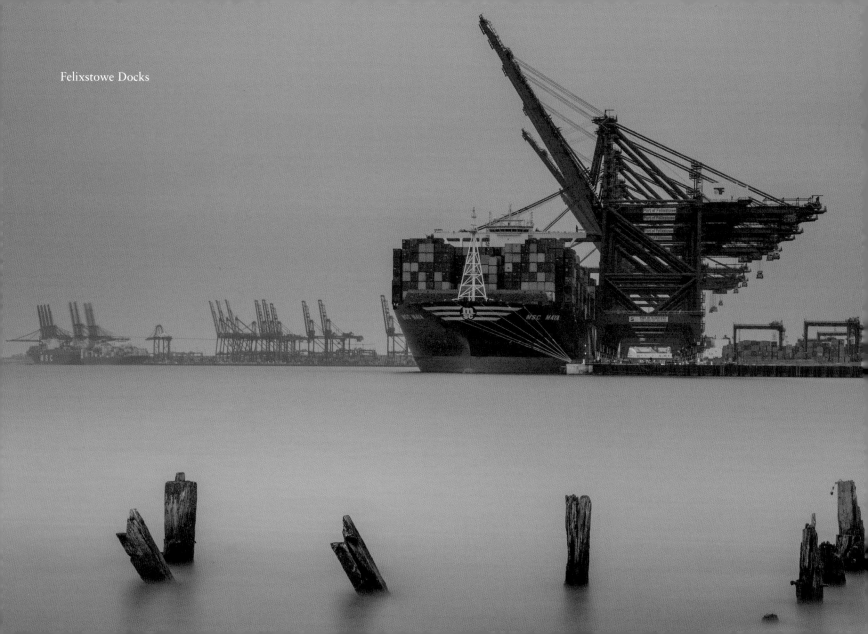

Felixstowe Docks

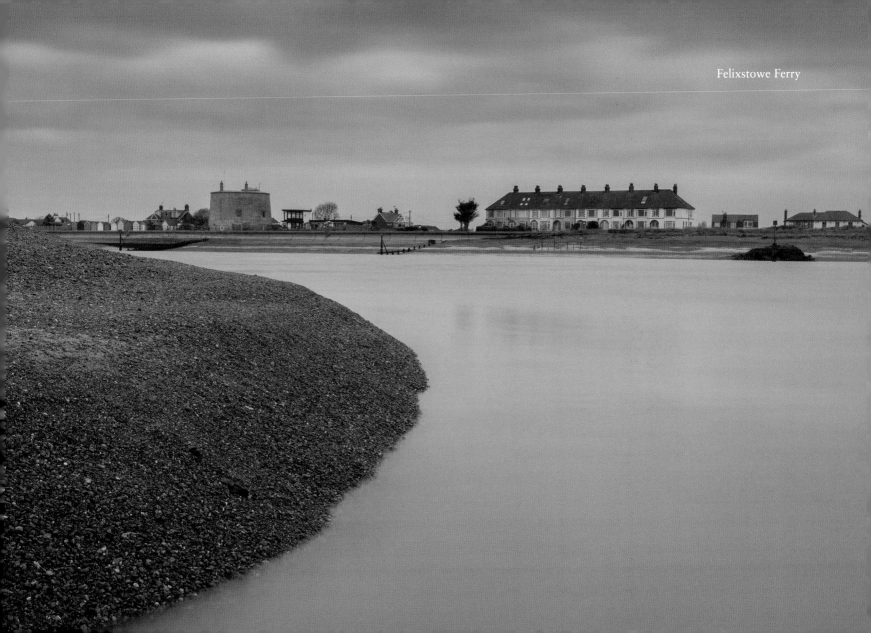

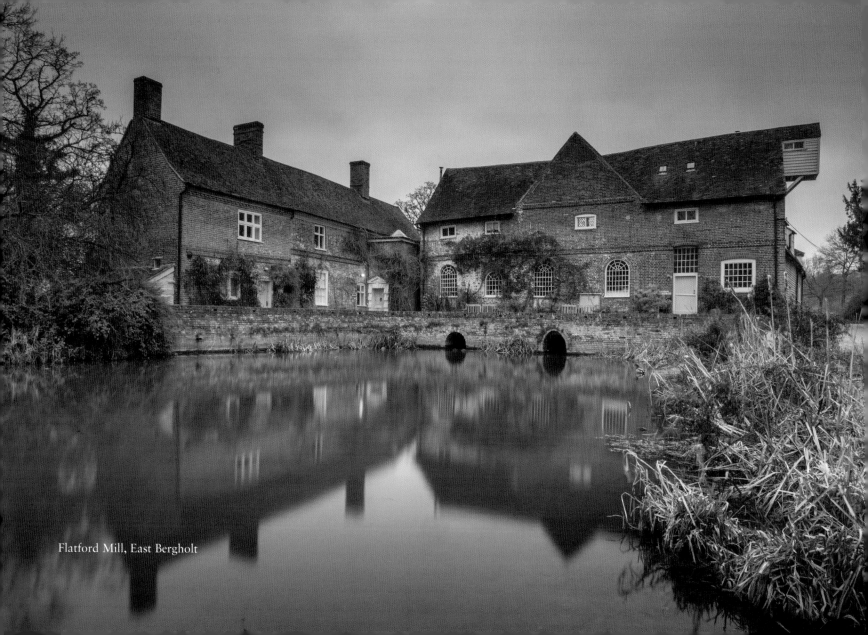

Flatford Mill, East Bergholt

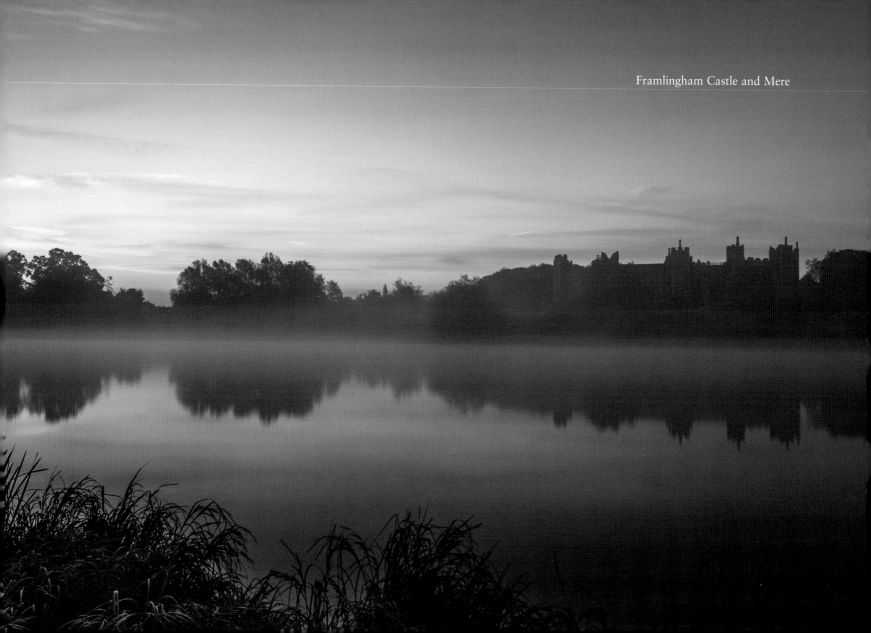

Framlingham Castle and Mere

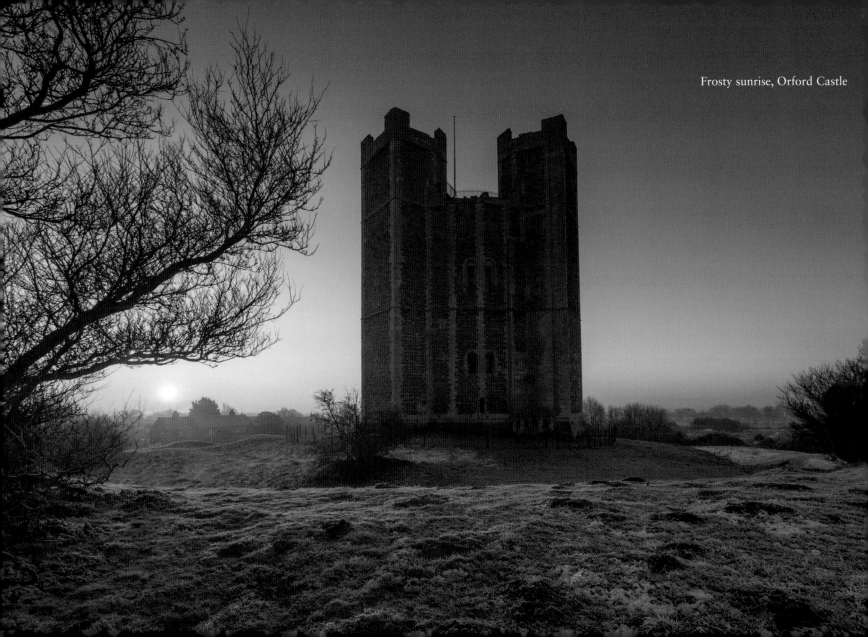

Frosty sunrise, Orford Castle

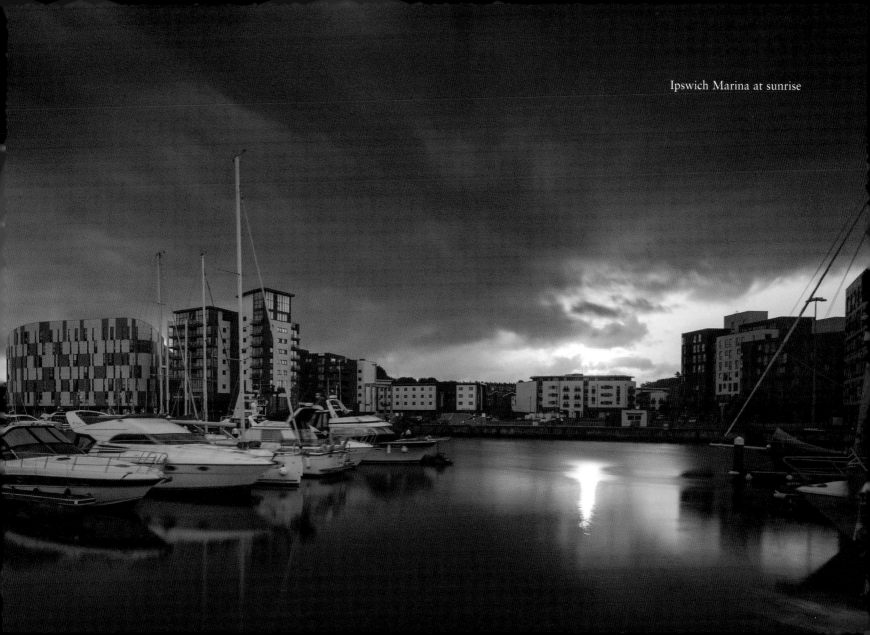
Ipswich Marina at sunrise

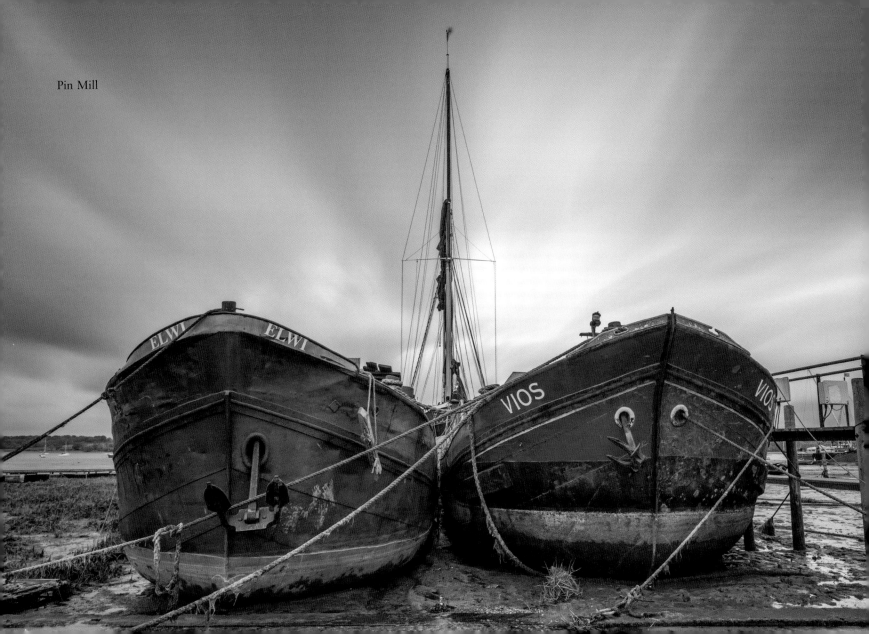

Pin Mill

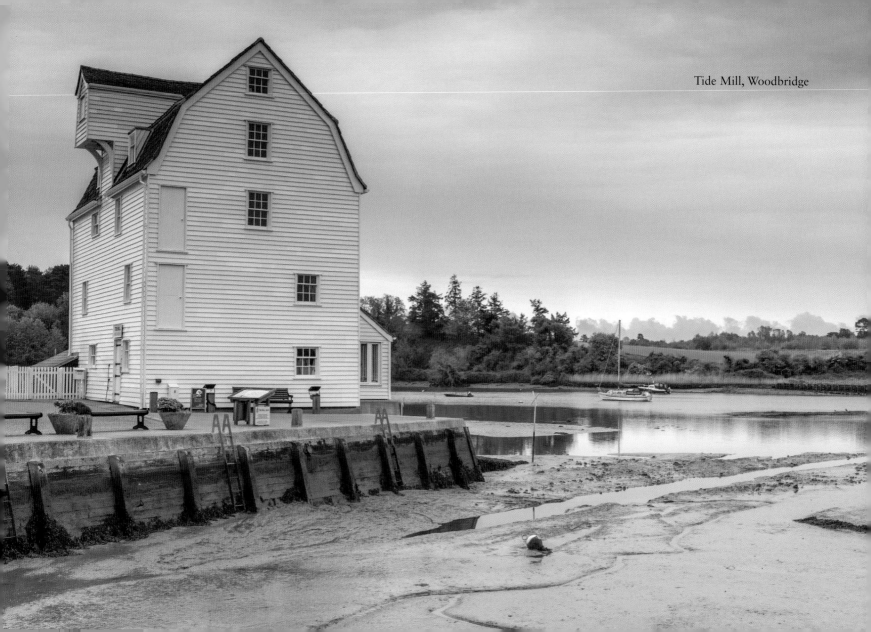

Tide Mill, Woodbridge

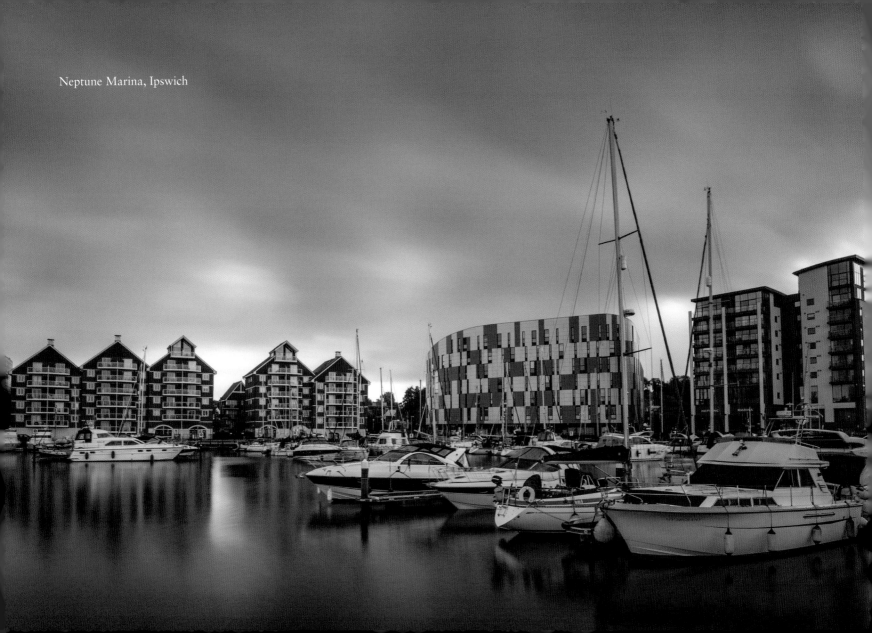

Neptune Marina, Ipswich

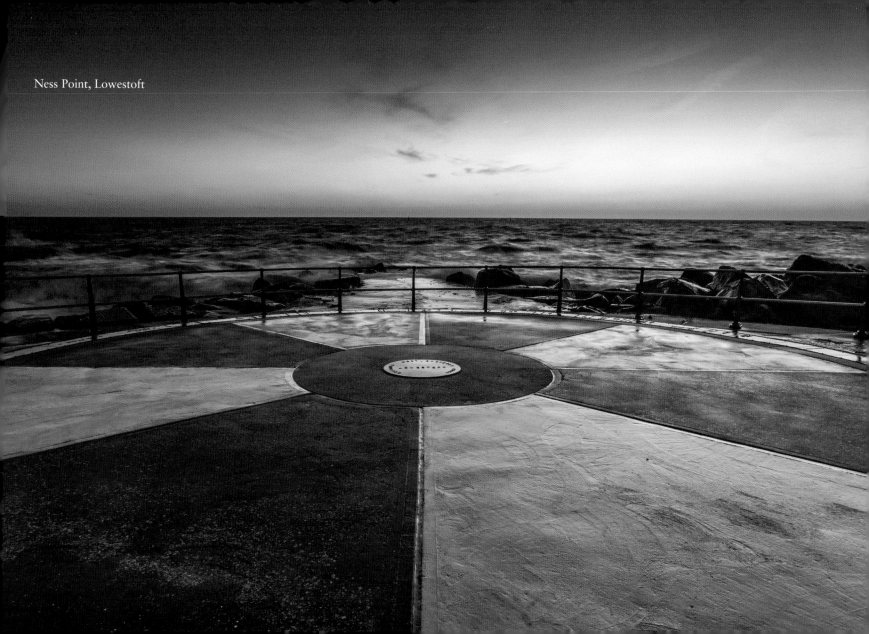

Ness Point, Lowestoft

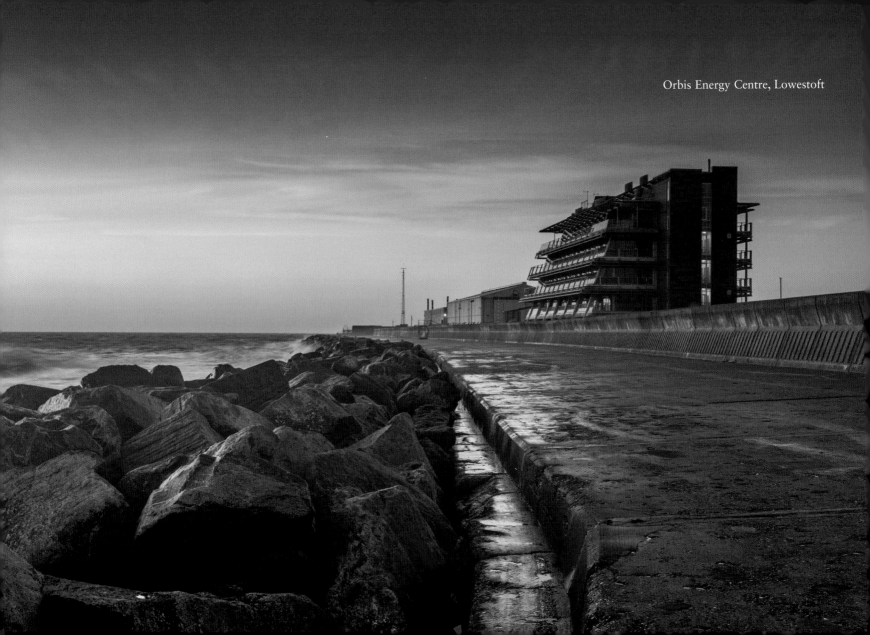

Orbis Energy Centre, Lowestoft

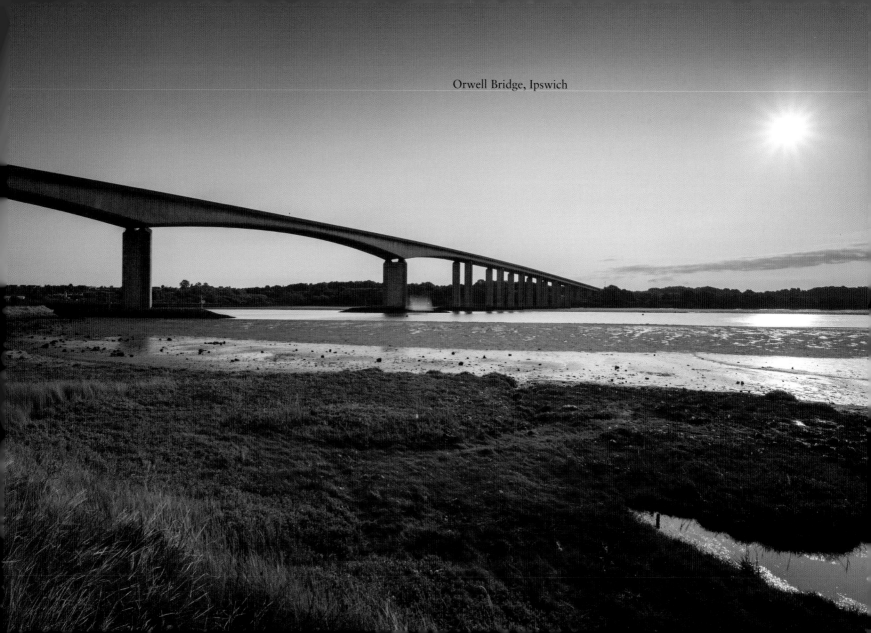
Orwell Bridge, Ipswich

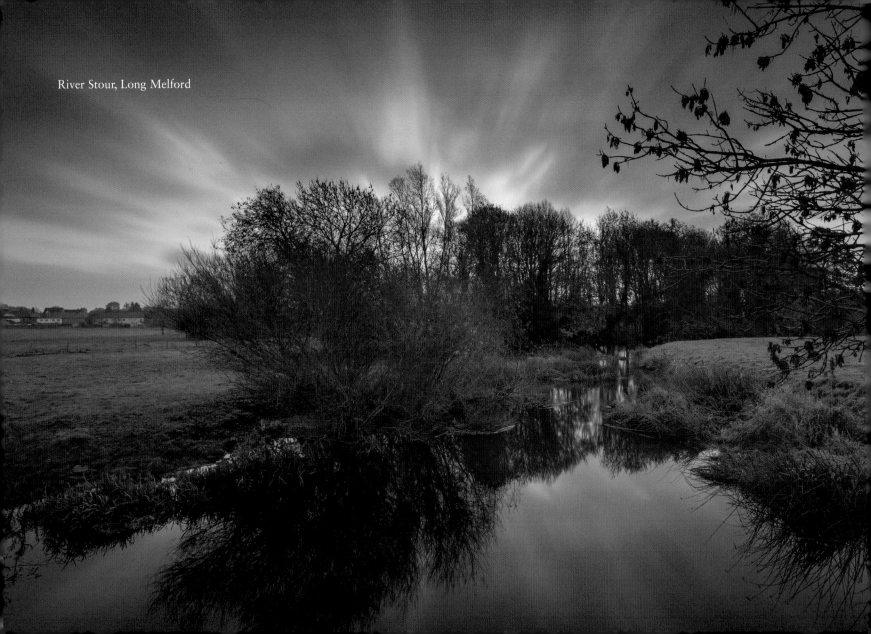

River Stour, Long Melford

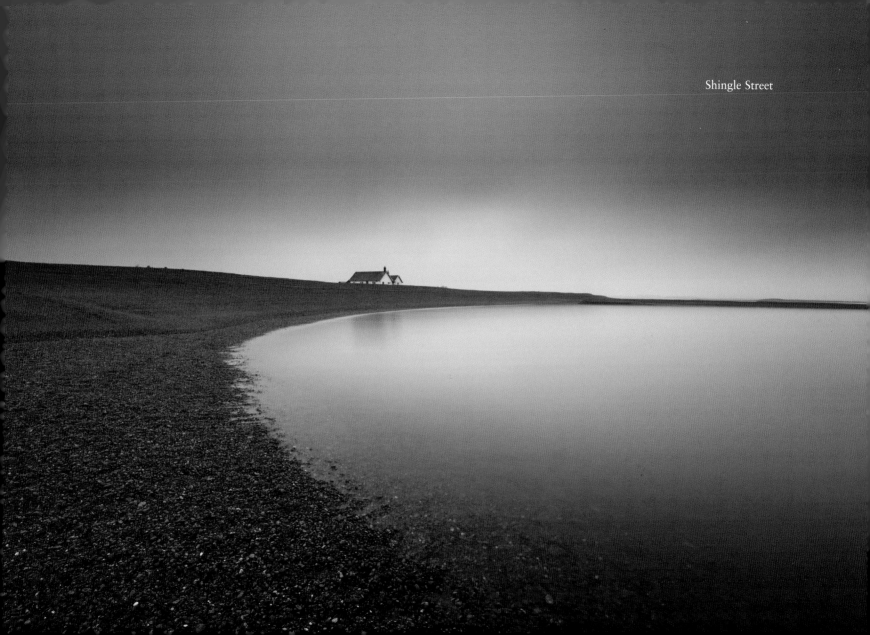

Shingle Street

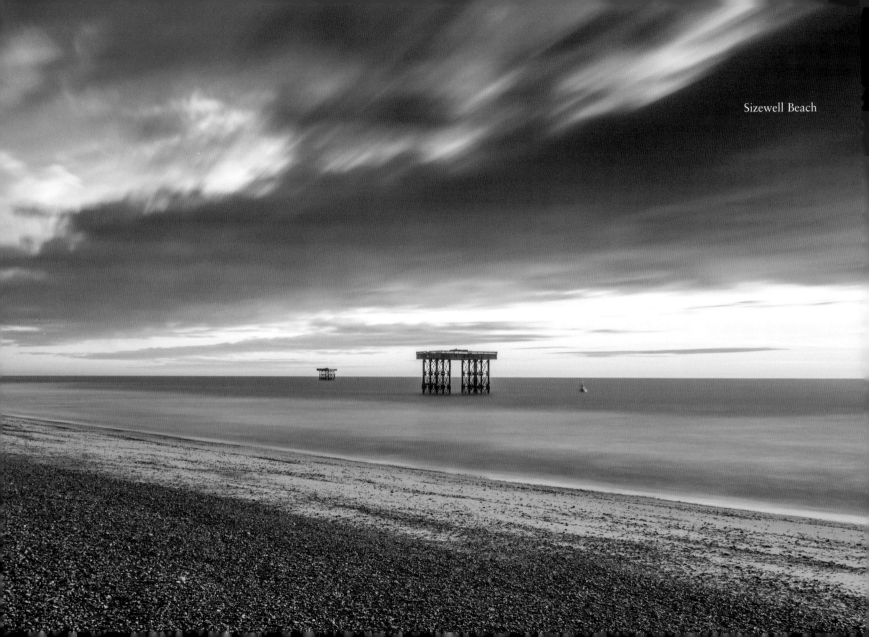

Sizewell Beach

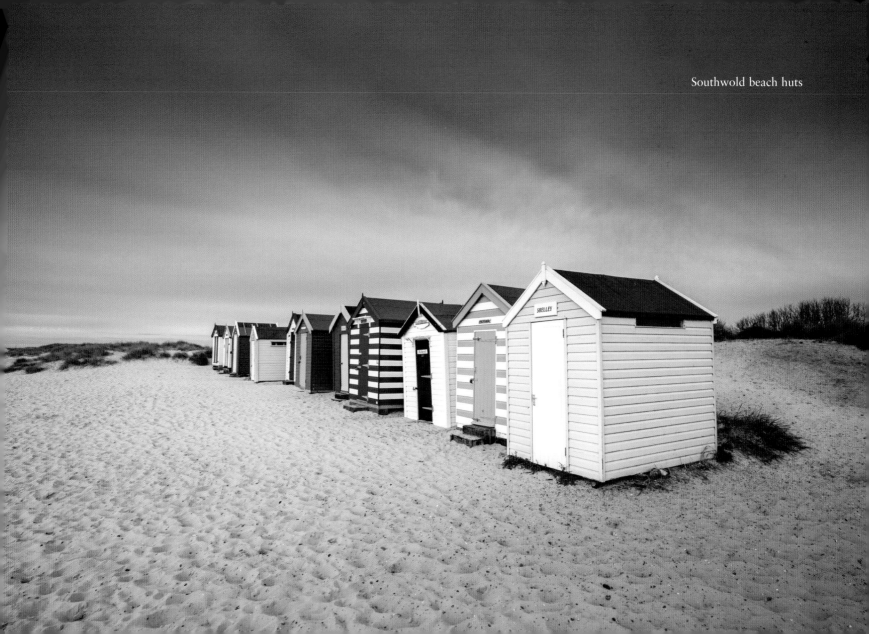

Southwold beach huts

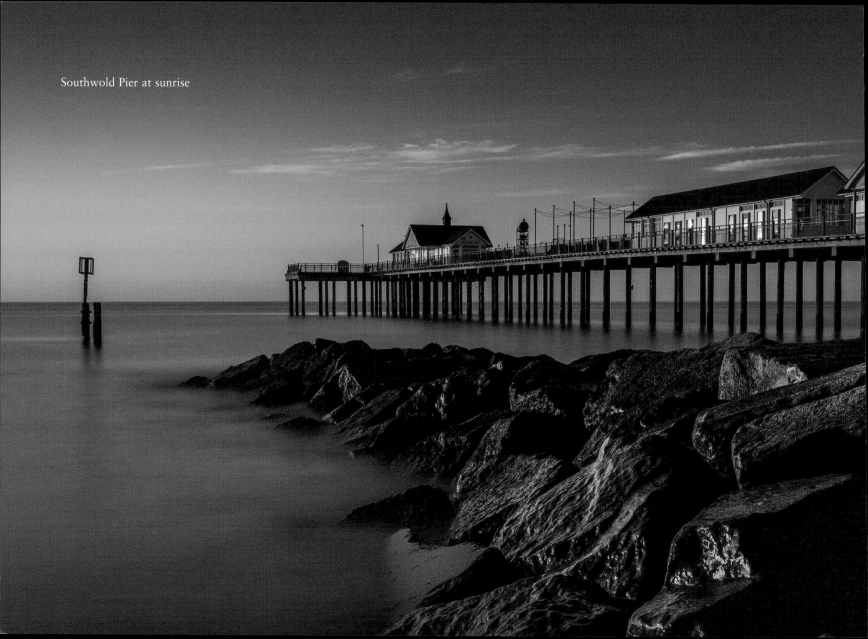
Southwold Pier at sunrise

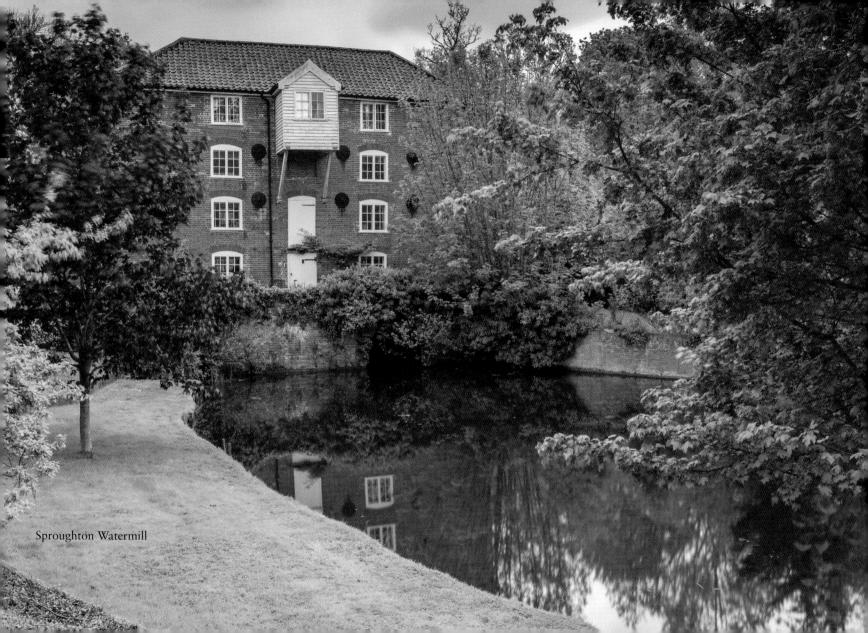

Sproughton Watermill

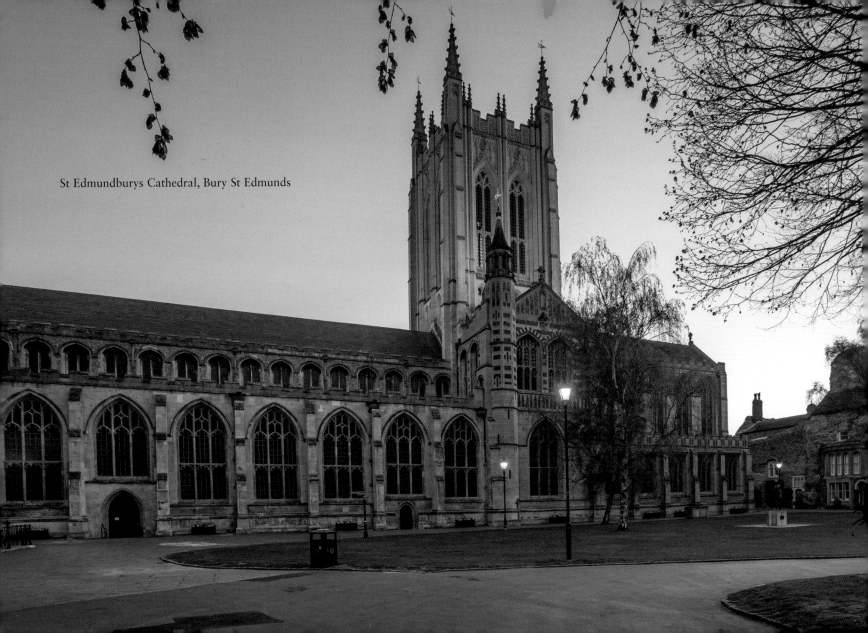

St Edmundburys Cathedral, Bury St Edmunds

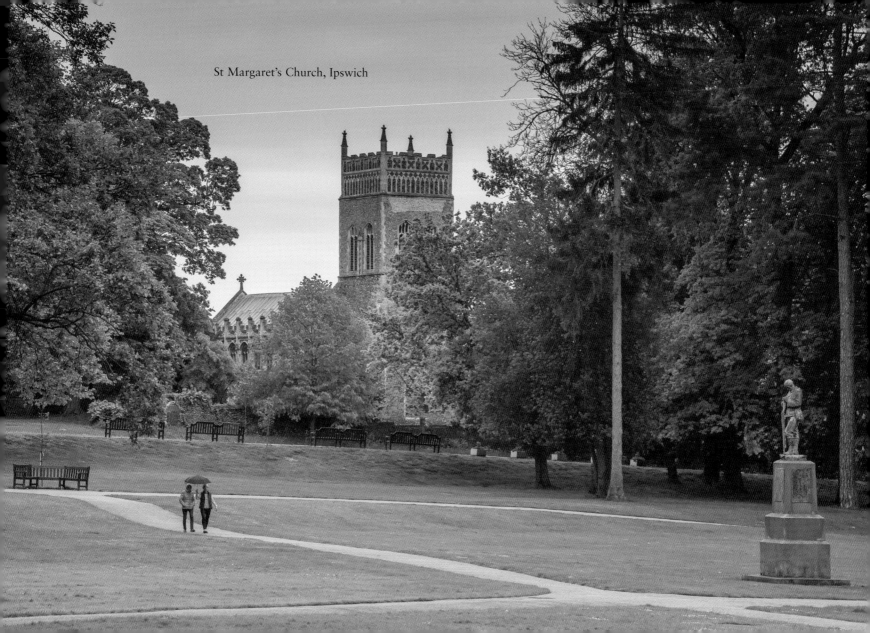

St Margaret's Church, Ipswich

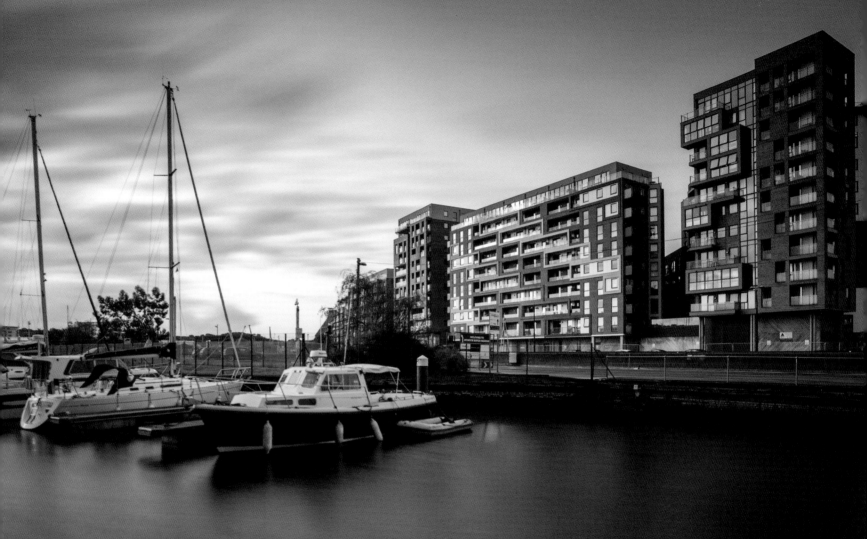

Stoke Quay, Ipswich

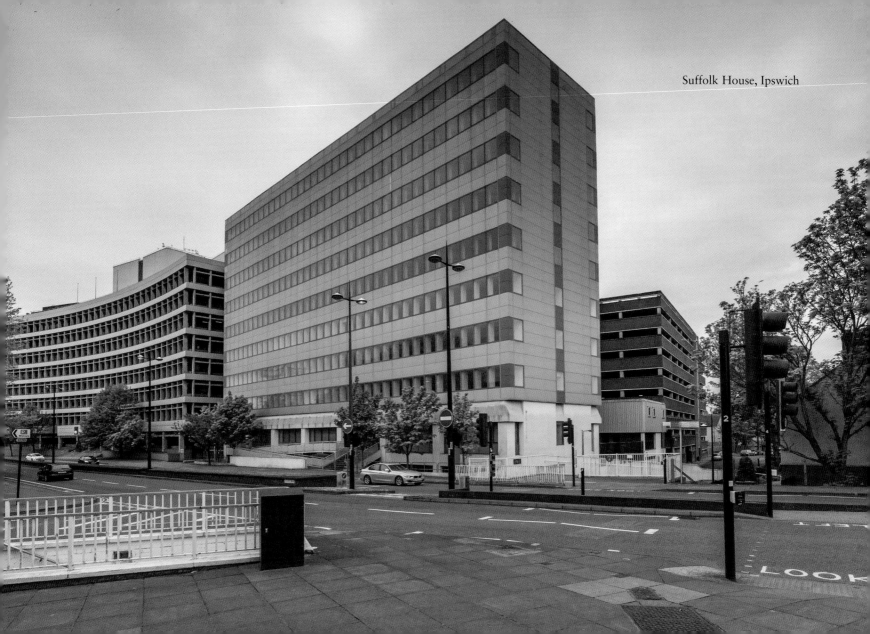

Suffolk House, Ipswich

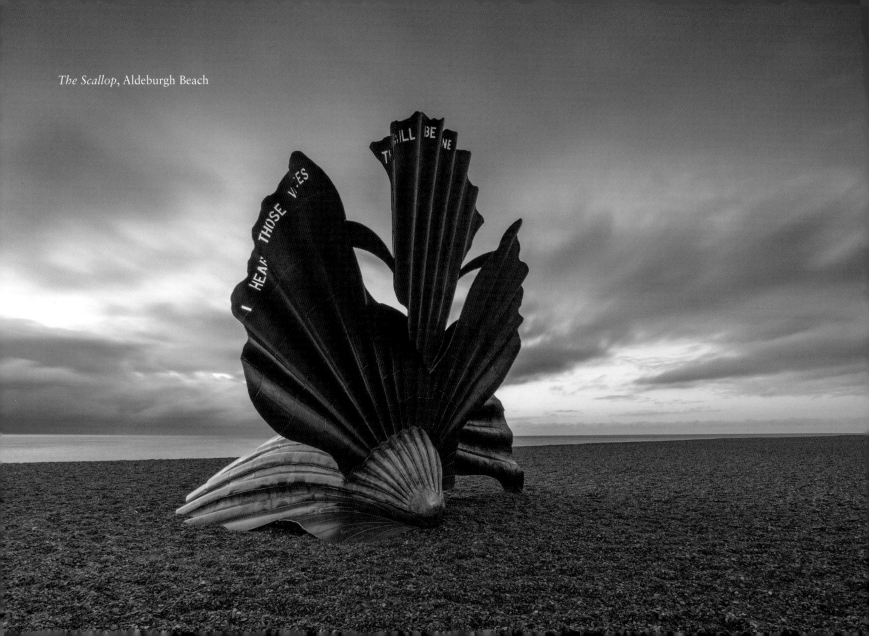

The Scallop, Aldeburgh Beach

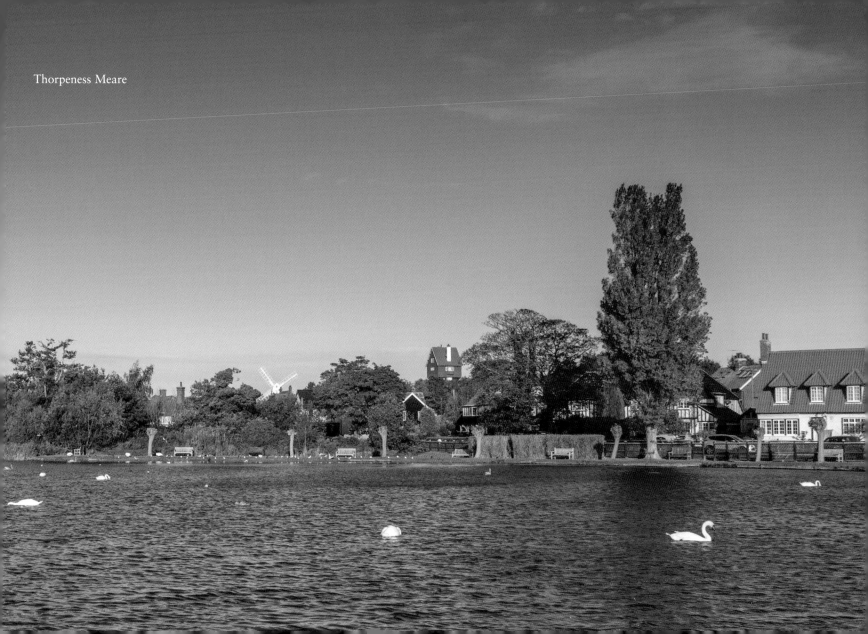

Thorpeness Meare

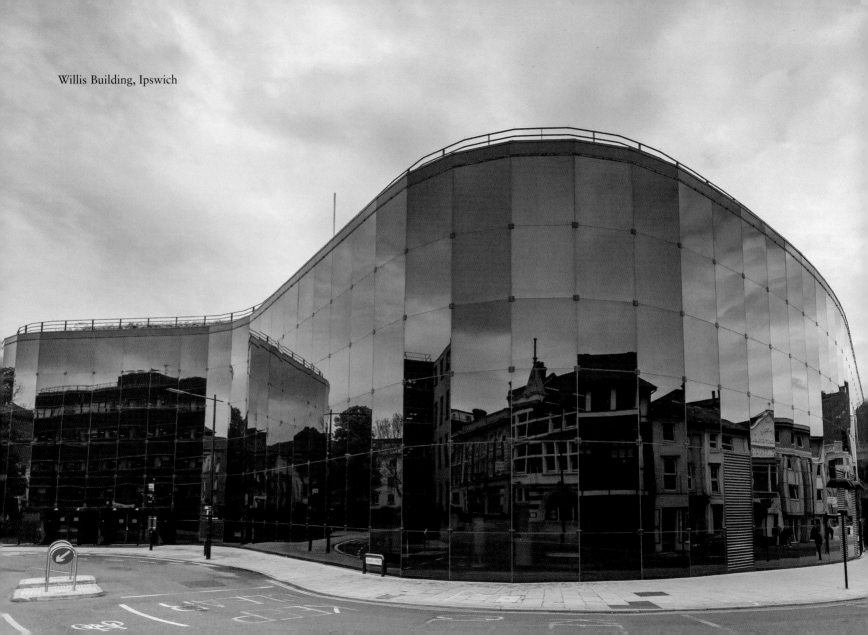

Willis Building, Ipswich

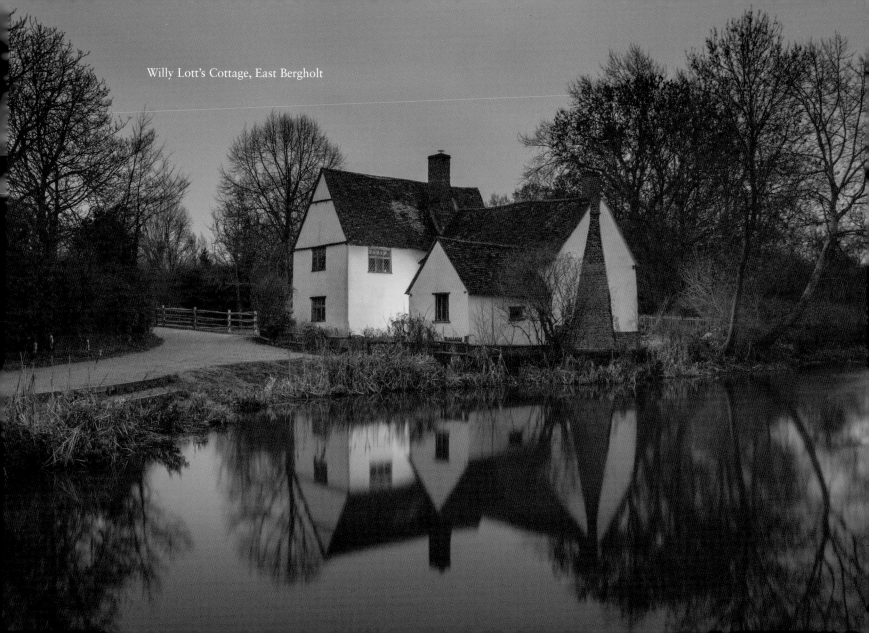

Willy Lott's Cottage, East Bergholt

CAMBRIDGESHIRE

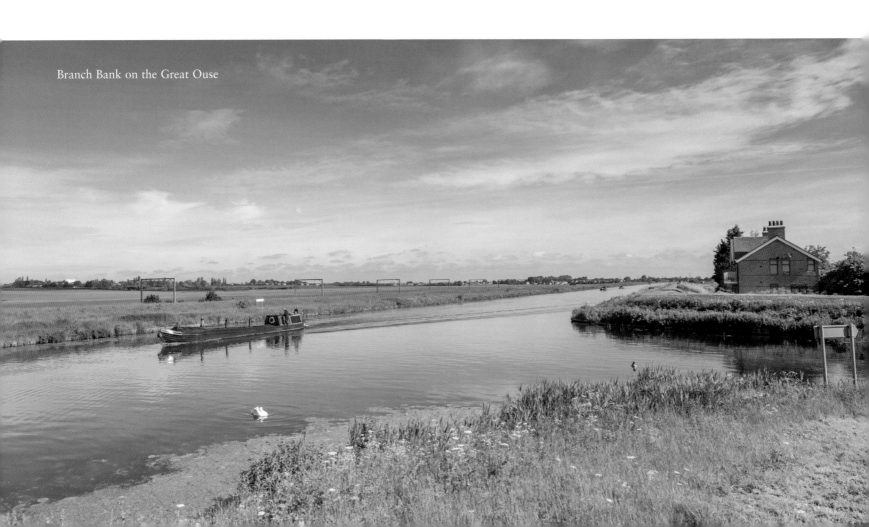

Branch Bank on the Great Ouse

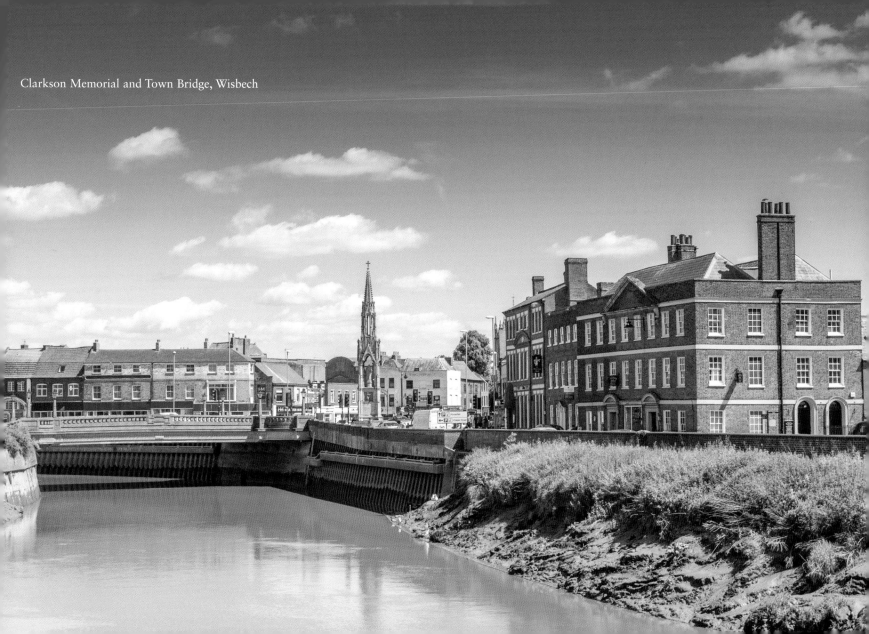

Clarkson Memorial and Town Bridge, Wisbech

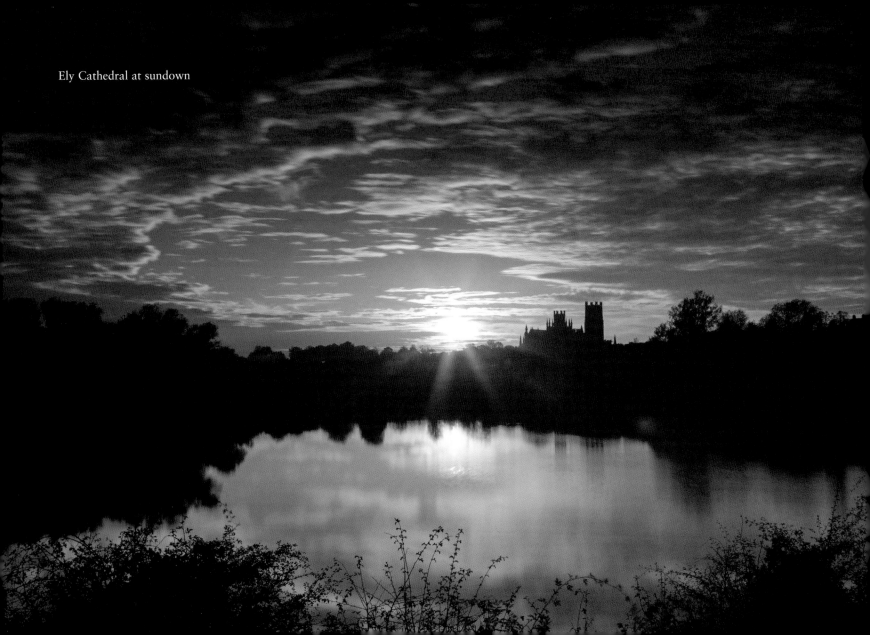

Ely Cathedral at sundown

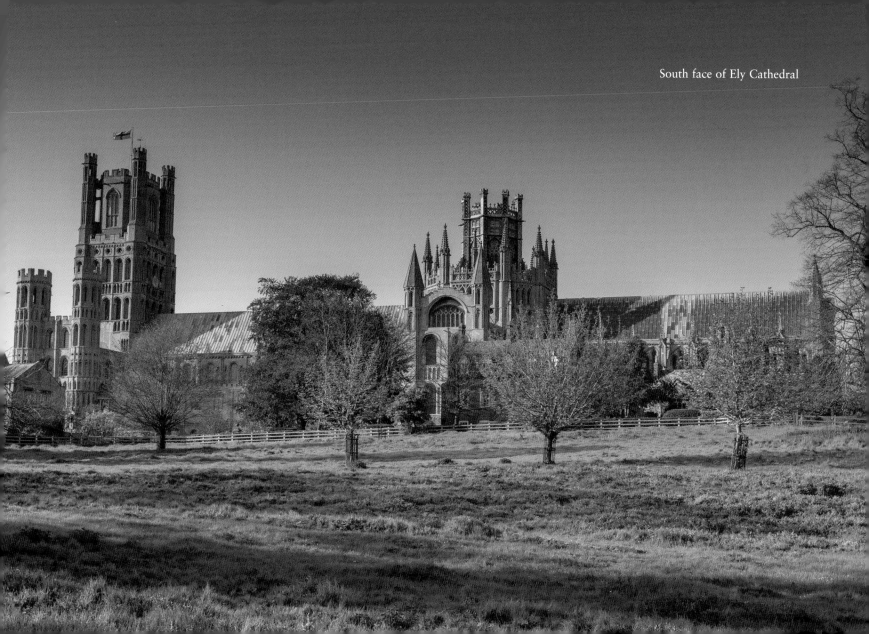

South face of Ely Cathedral

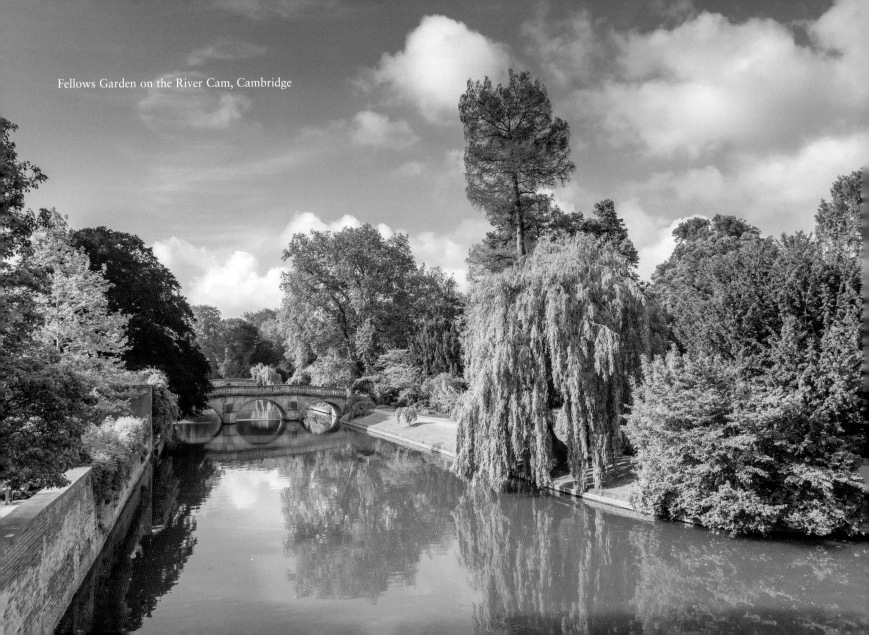

Fellows Garden on the River Cam, Cambridge

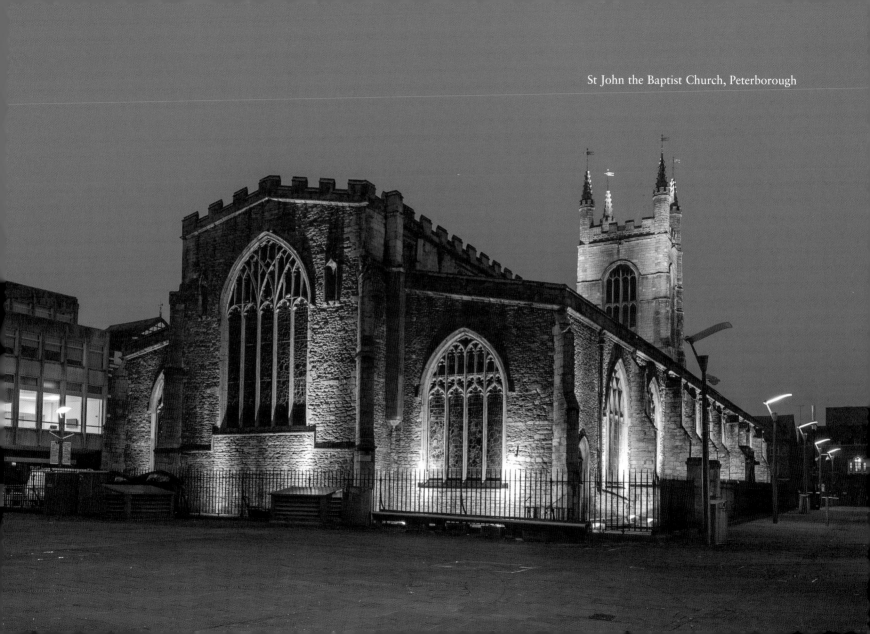

St John the Baptist Church, Peterborough

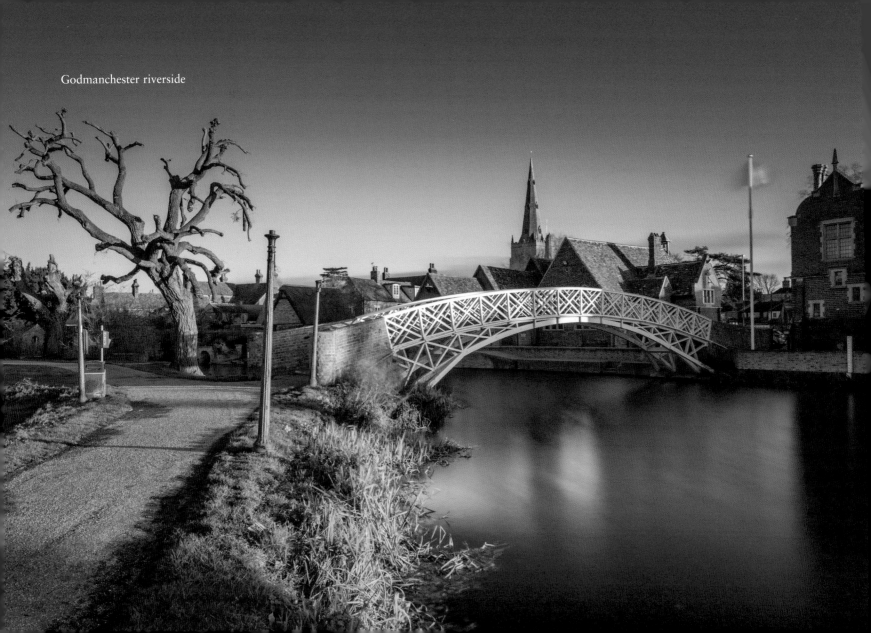

Godmanchester riverside

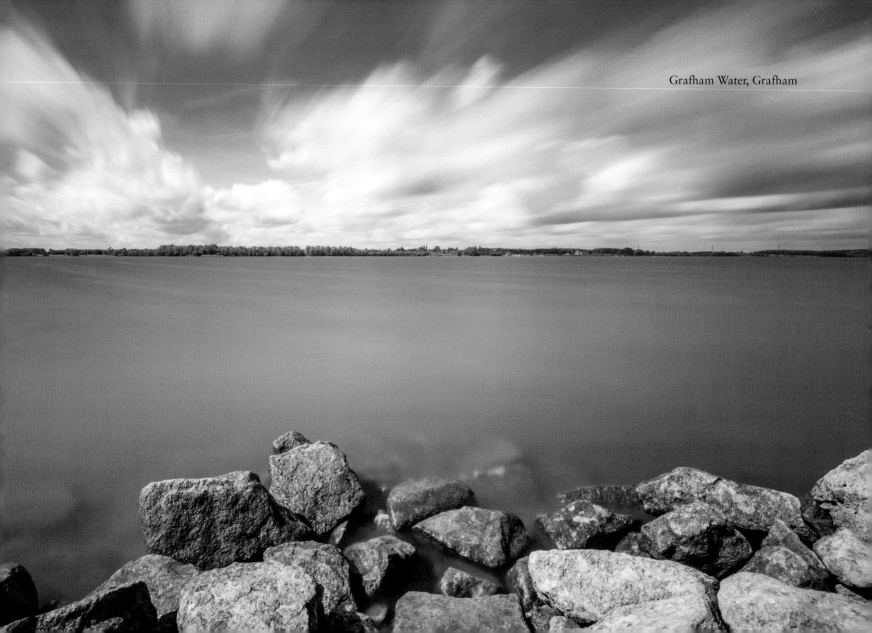

Grafham Water, Grafham

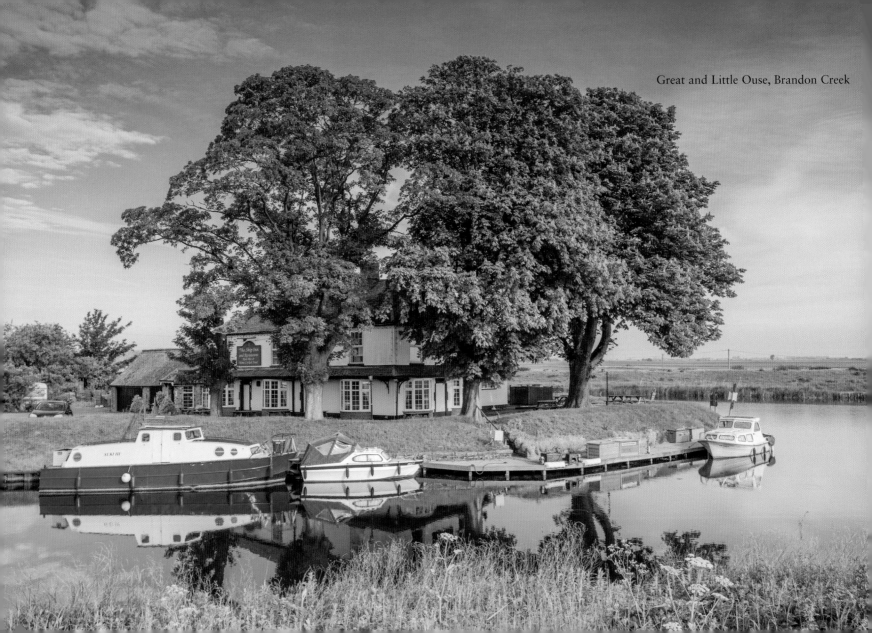

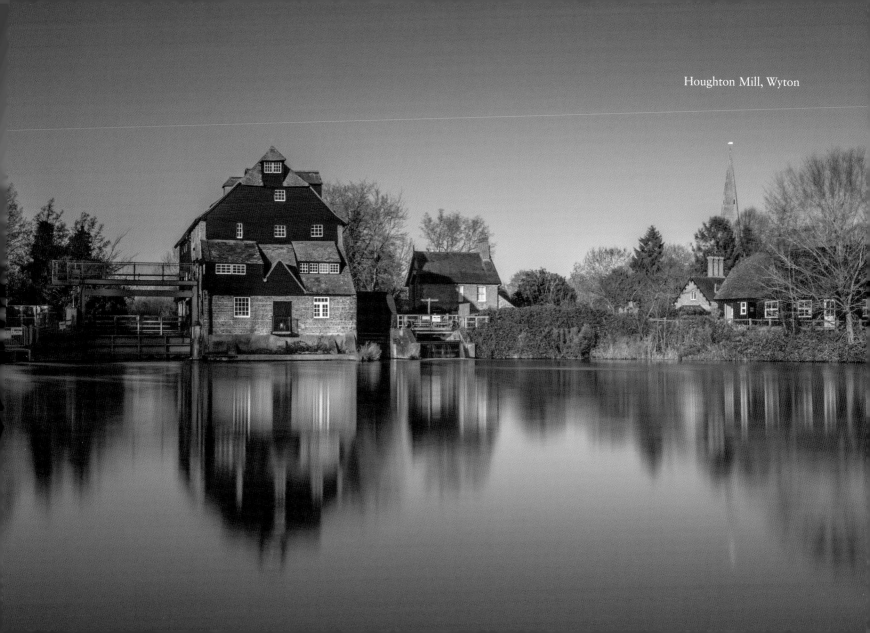

Houghton Mill, Wyton

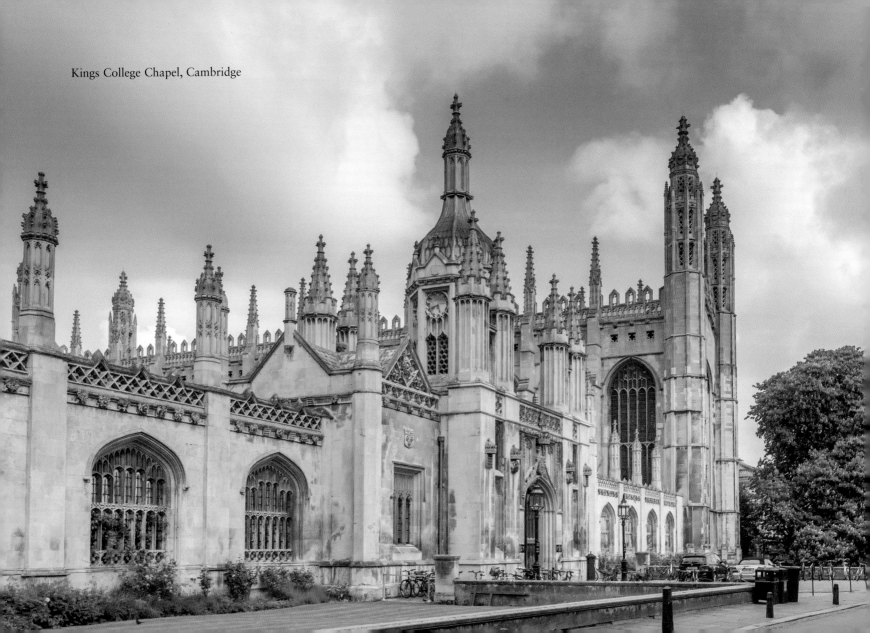

Kings College Chapel, Cambridge

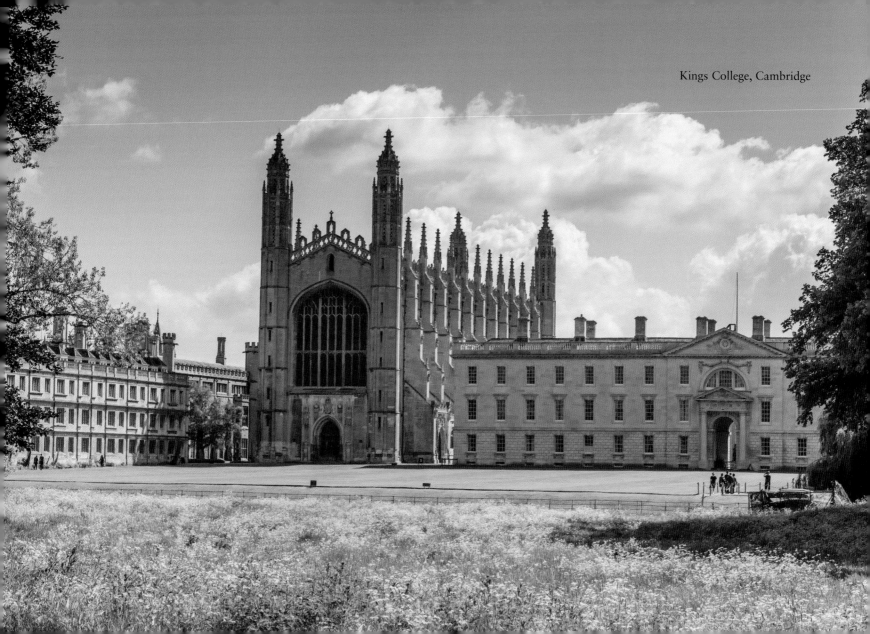

Kings College, Cambridge

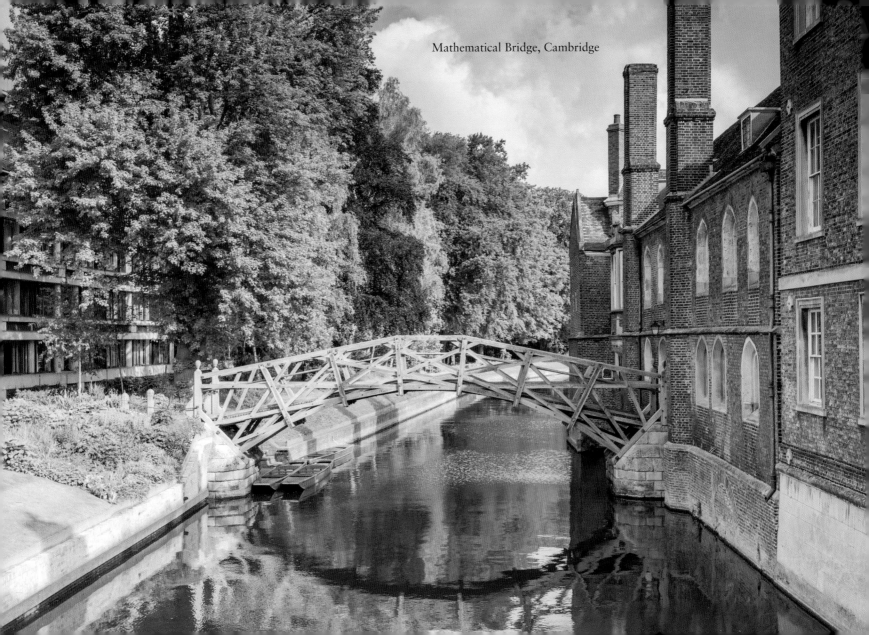

Mathematical Bridge, Cambridge

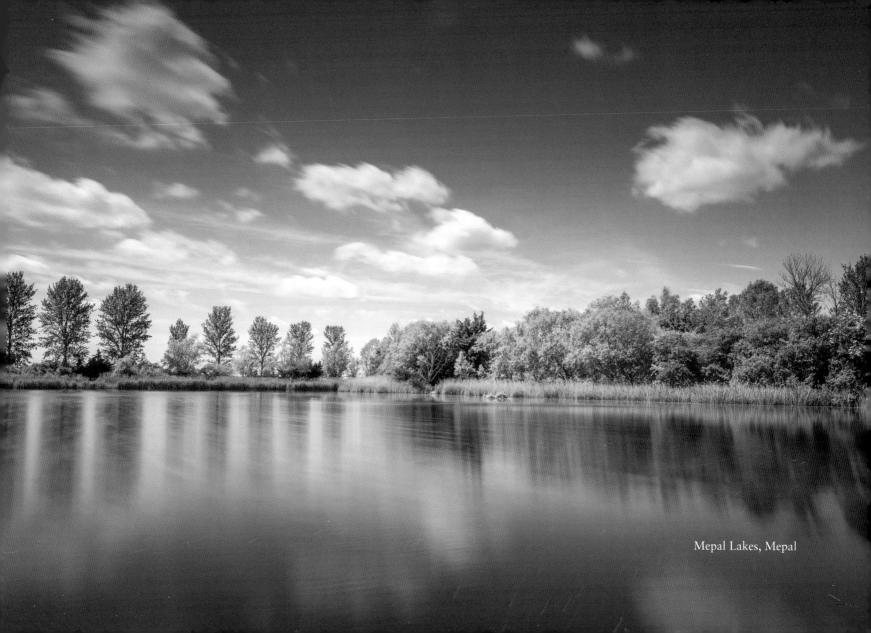

Mepal Lakes, Mepal

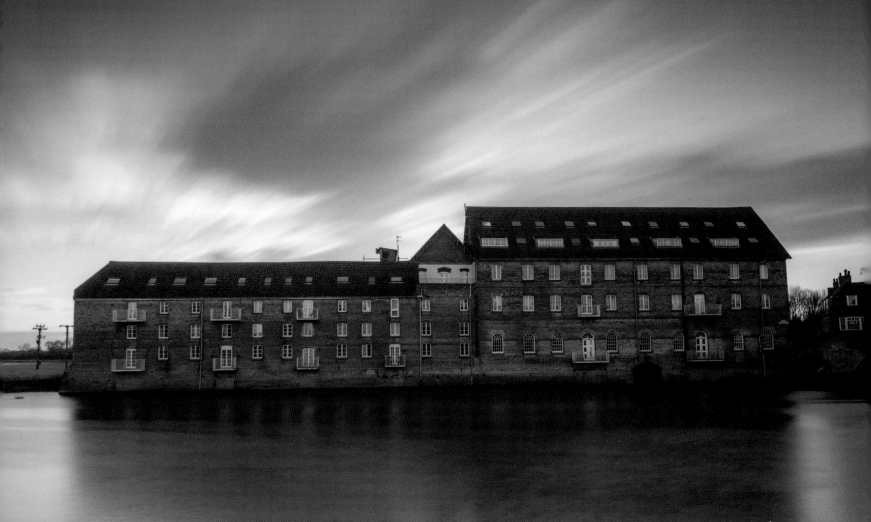

Mill on the Great Ouse, Huntingdon

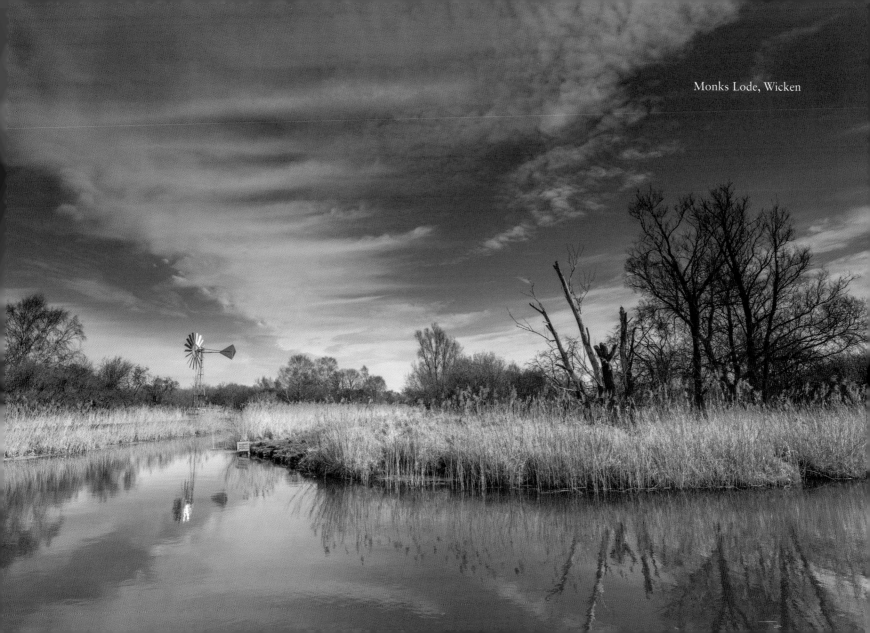

Monks Lode, Wicken

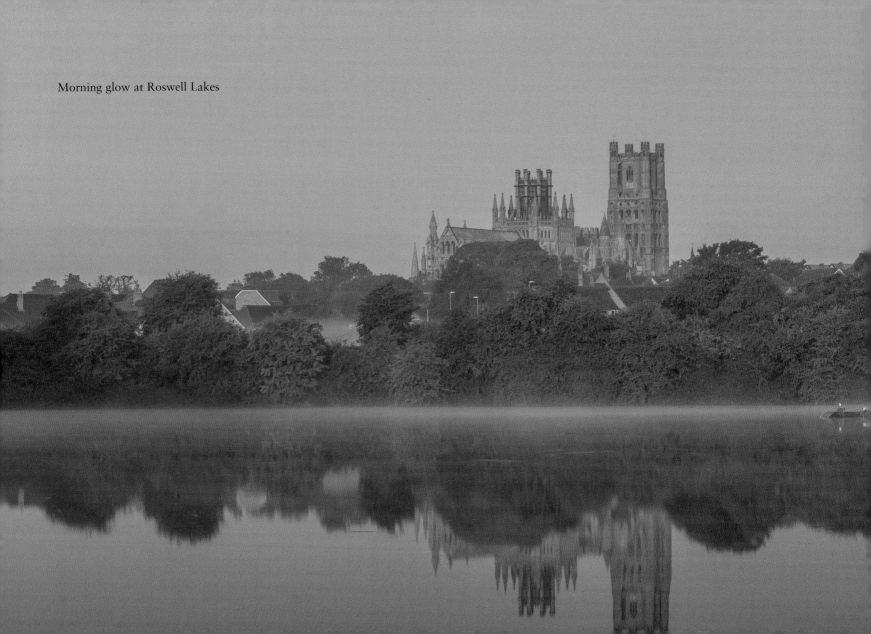

Morning glow at Roswell Lakes

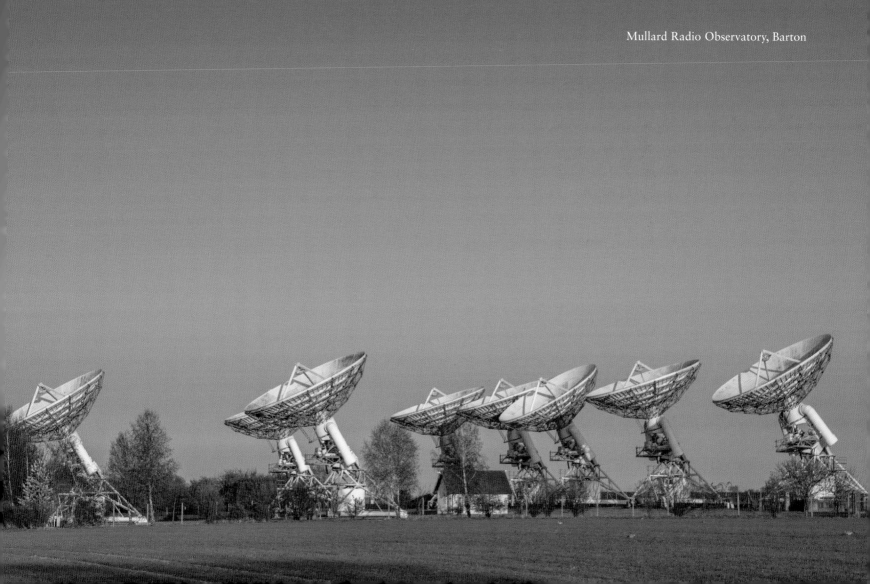

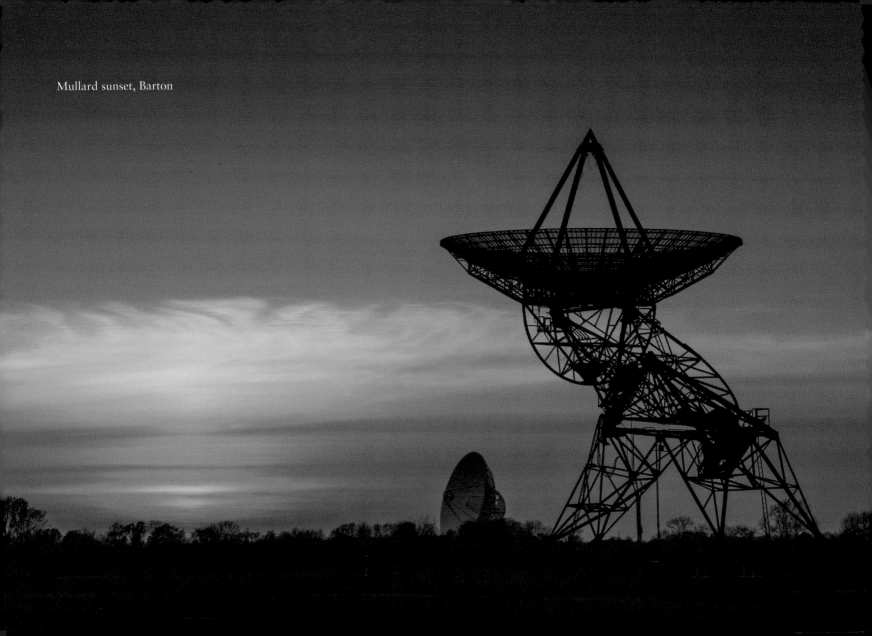

Mullard sunset, Barton

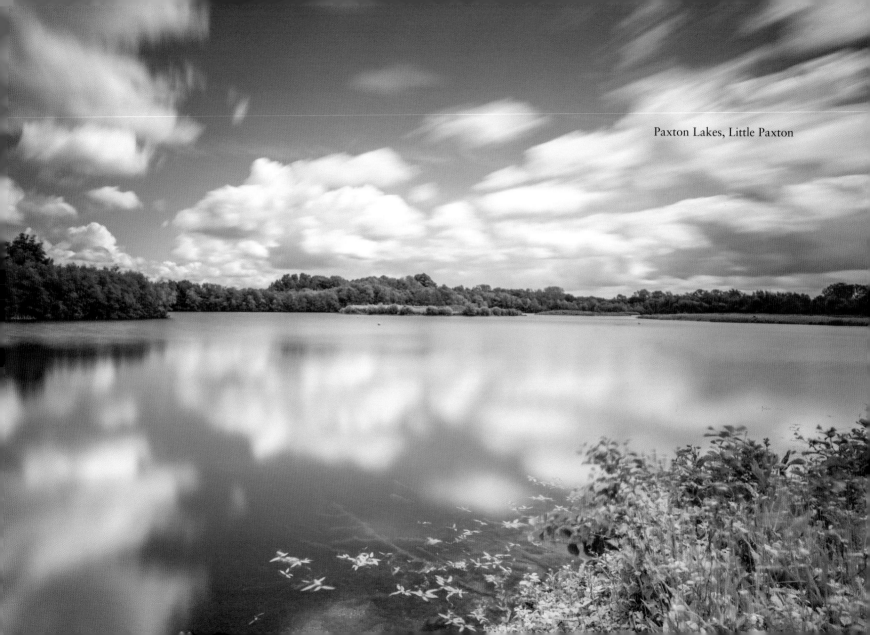

Paxton Lakes, Little Paxton

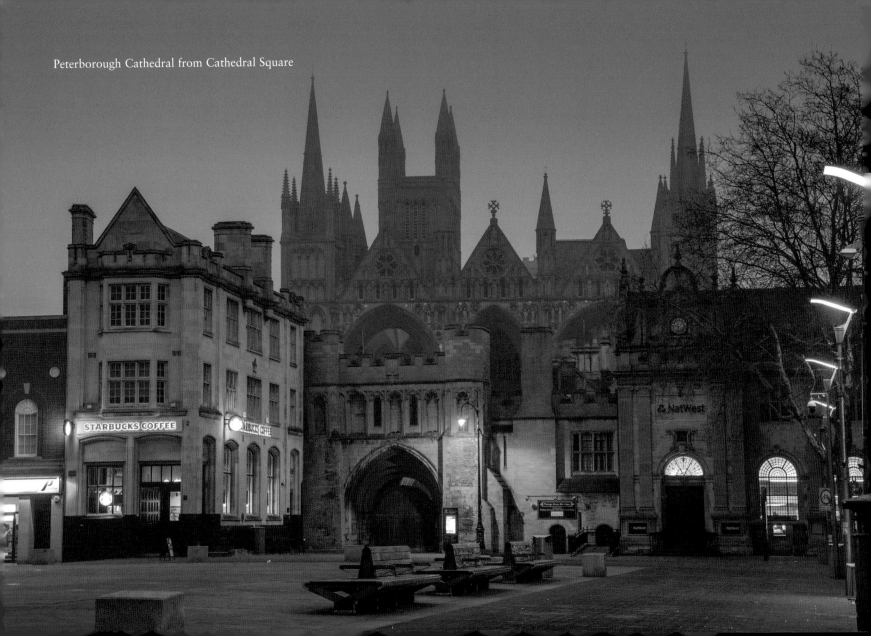

Peterborough Cathedral from Cathedral Square

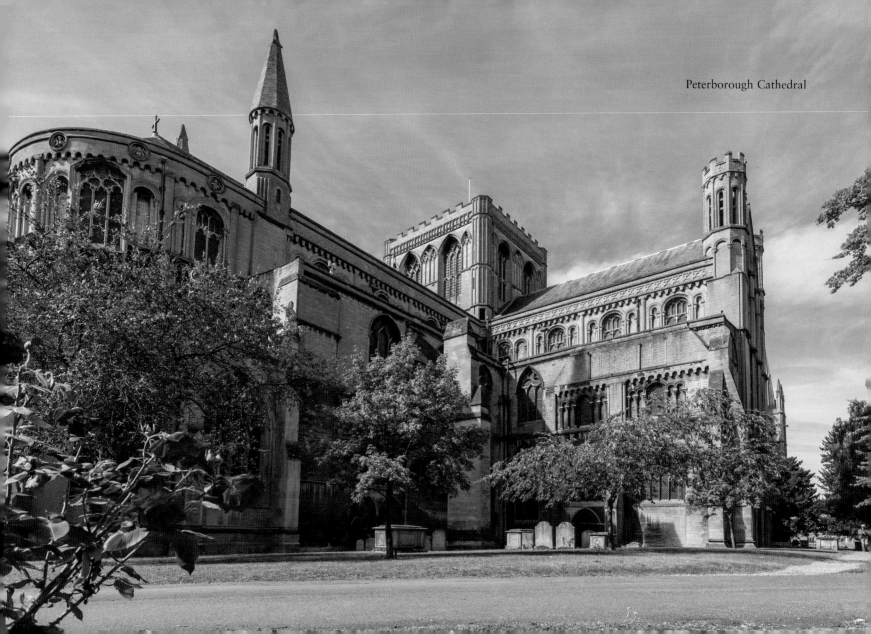

Peterborough Cathedral

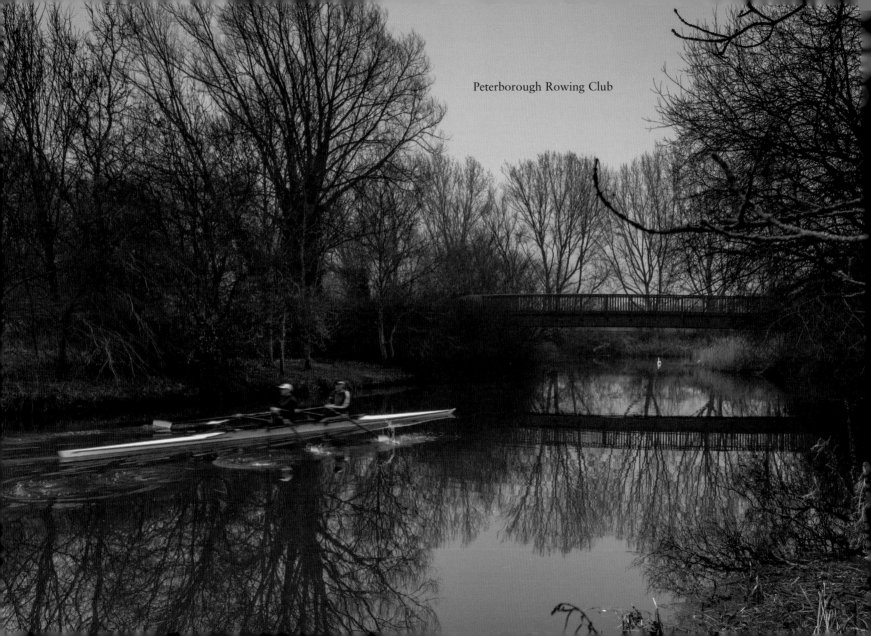

Peterborough Rowing Club

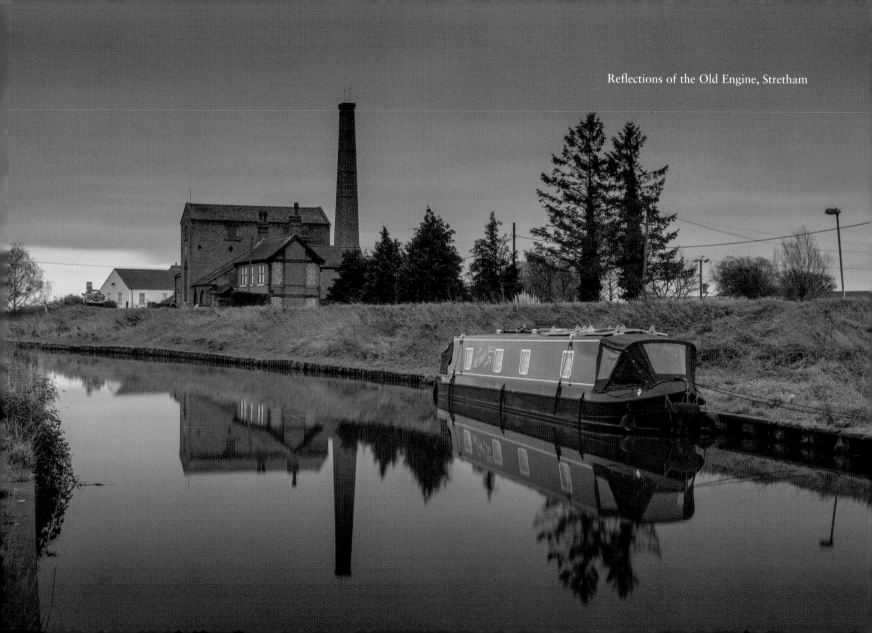

Reflections of the Old Engine, Stretham

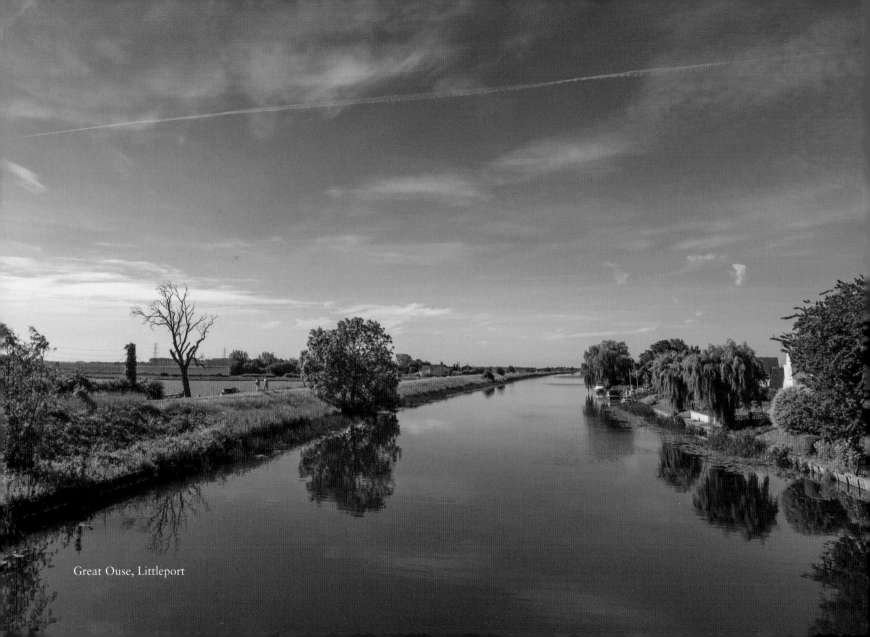

Great Ouse, Littleport

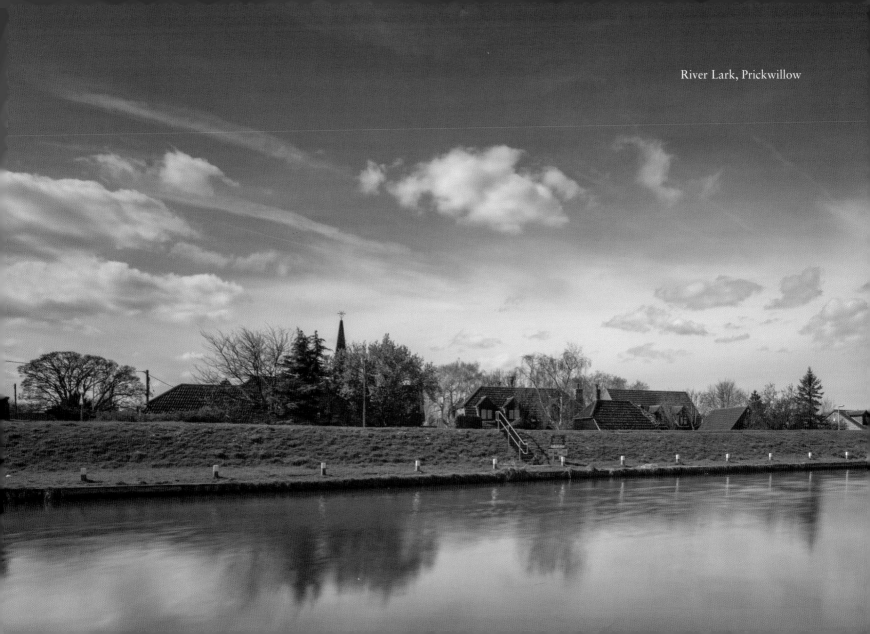

River Lark, Prickwillow

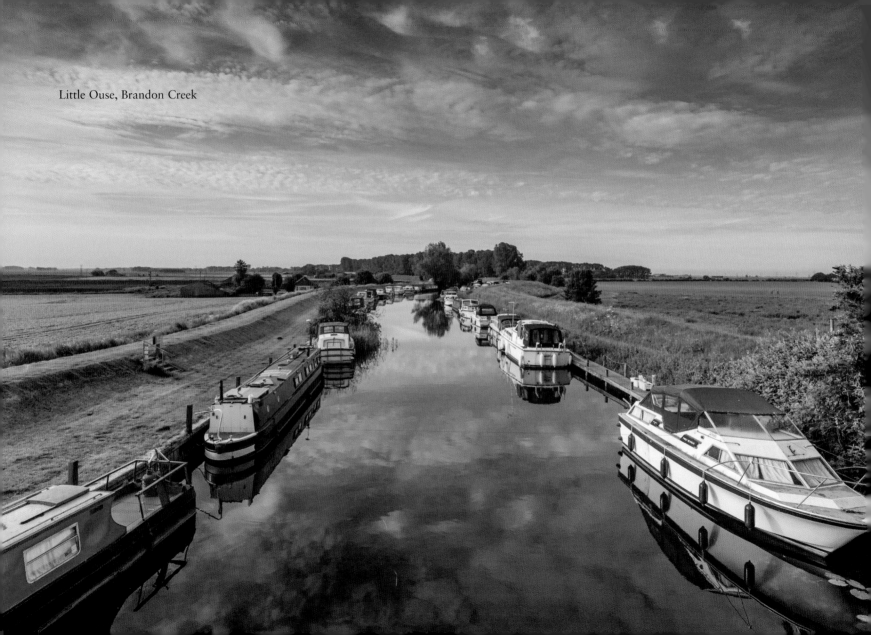

Little Ouse, Brandon Creek

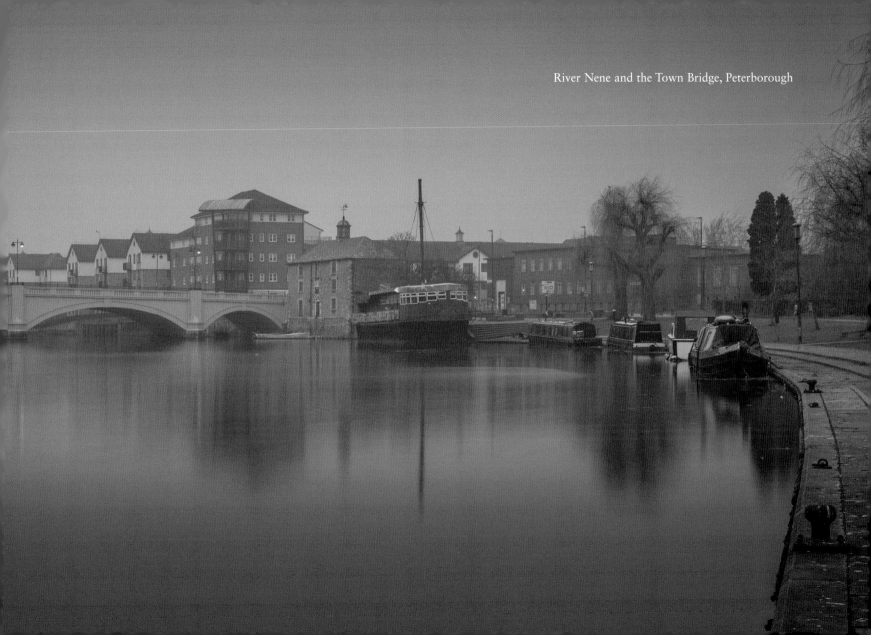

River Nene and the Town Bridge, Peterborough

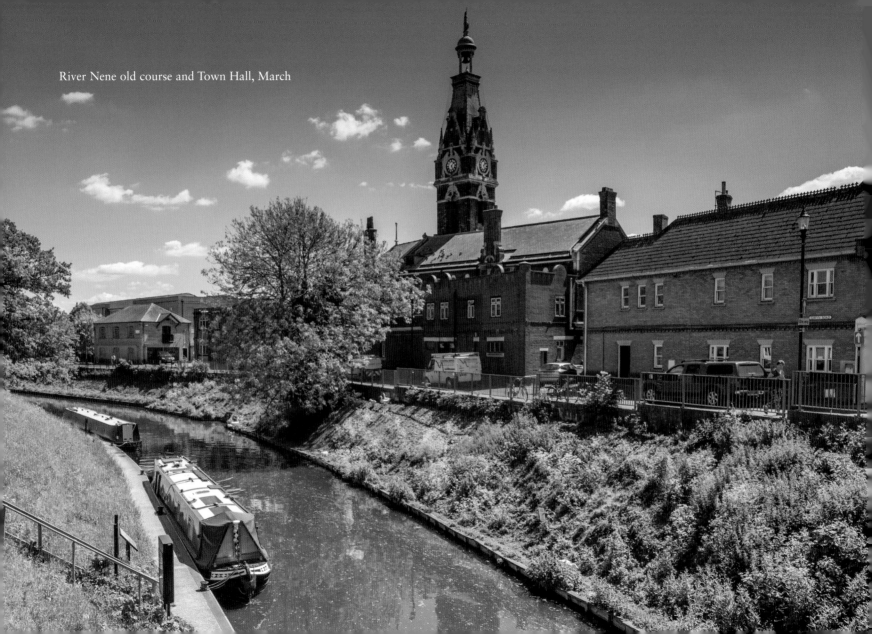
River Nene old course and Town Hall, March

Great Ouse, St Neots

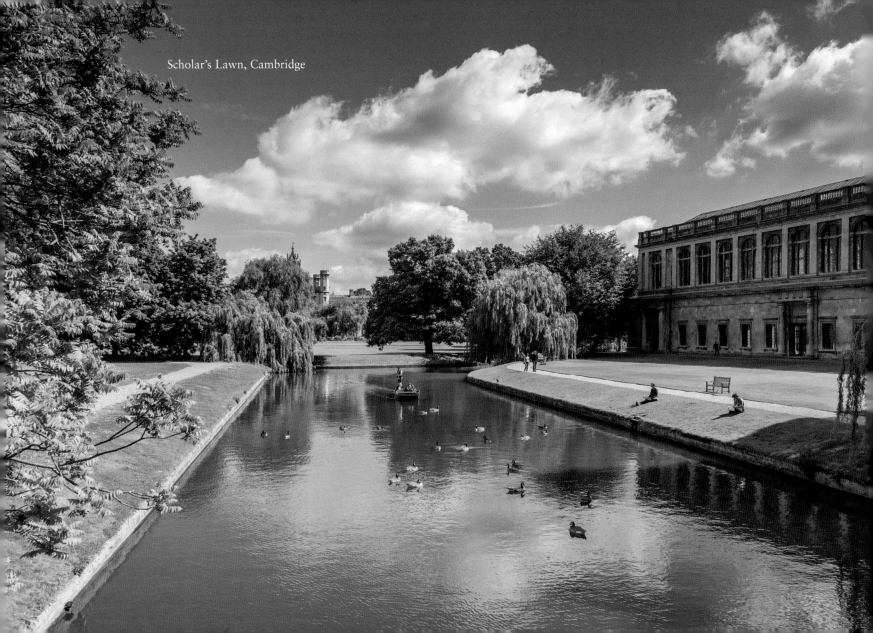

Scholar's Lawn, Cambridge

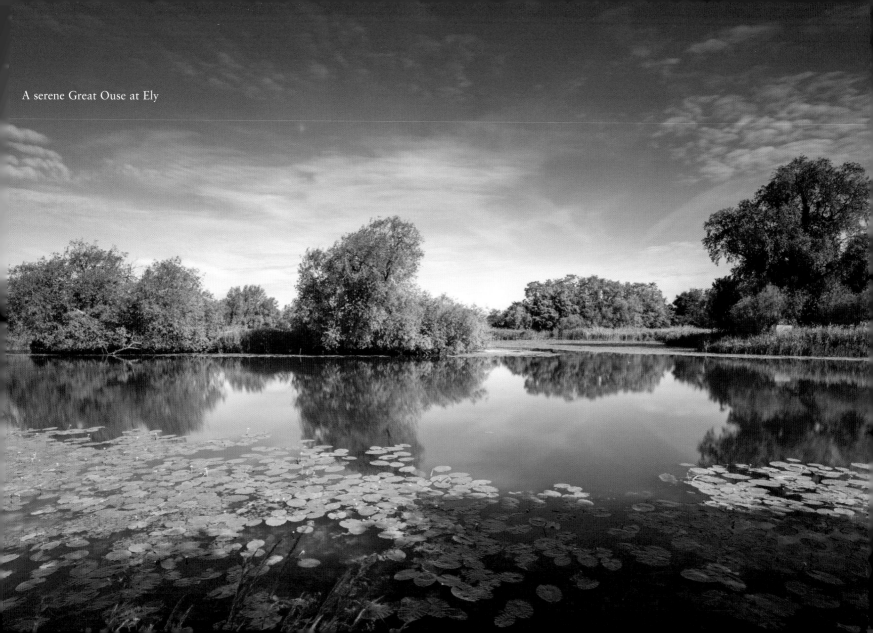

A serene Great Ouse at Ely

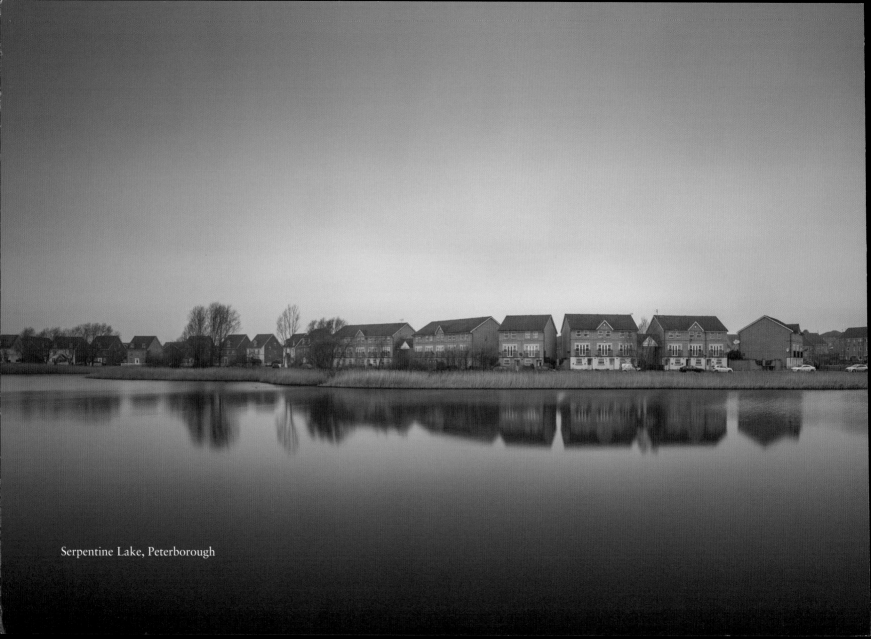

Serpentine Lake, Peterborough

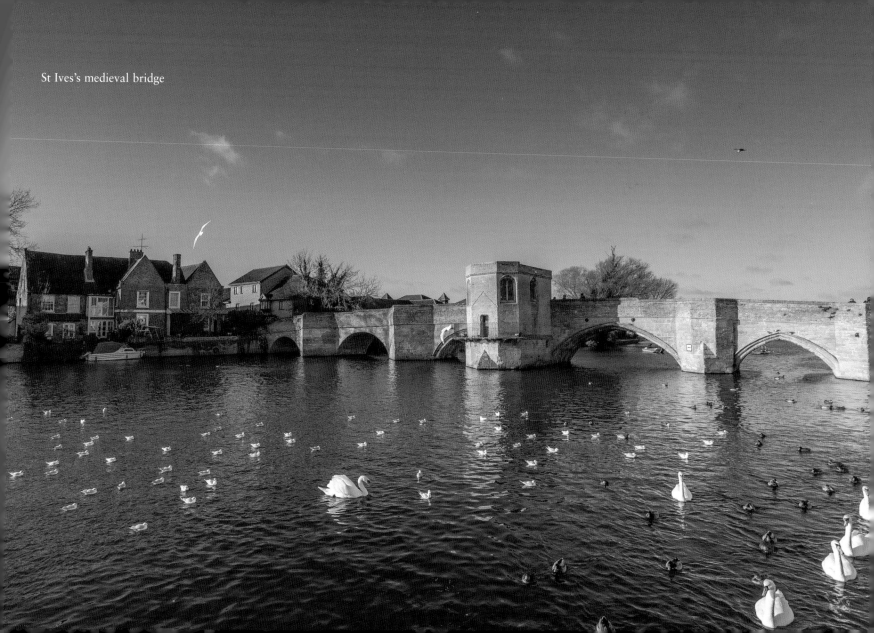

St Ives's medieval bridge

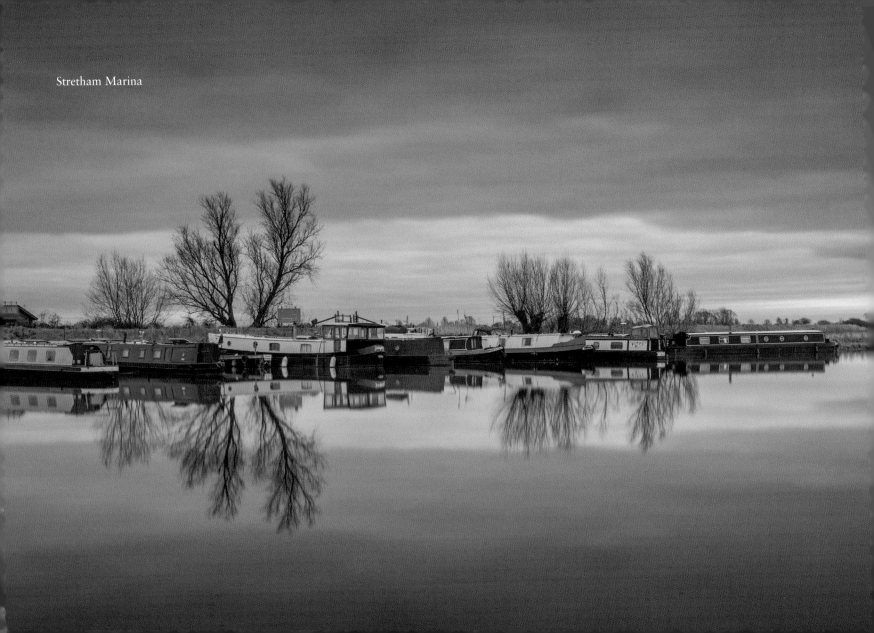

Stretham Marina

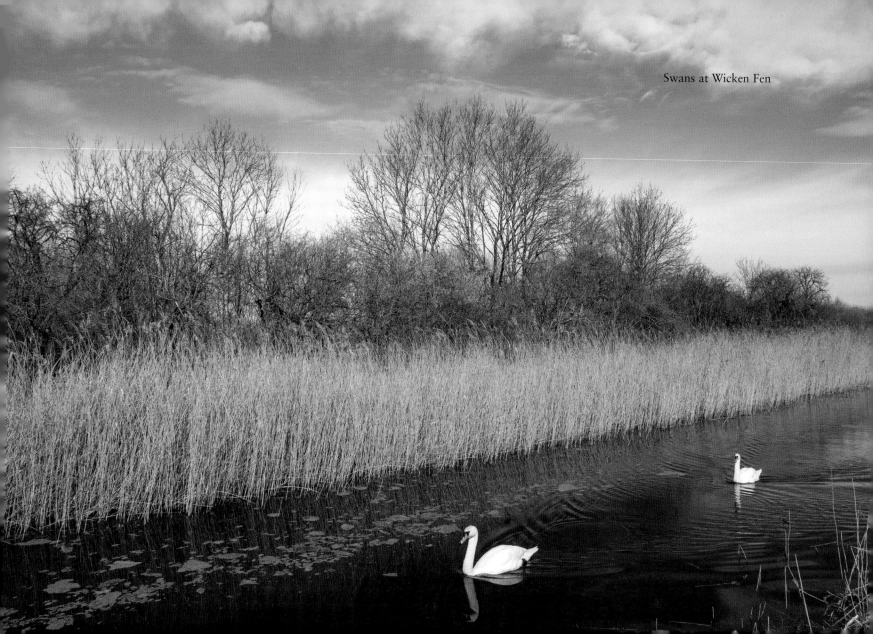

Swans at Wicken Fen

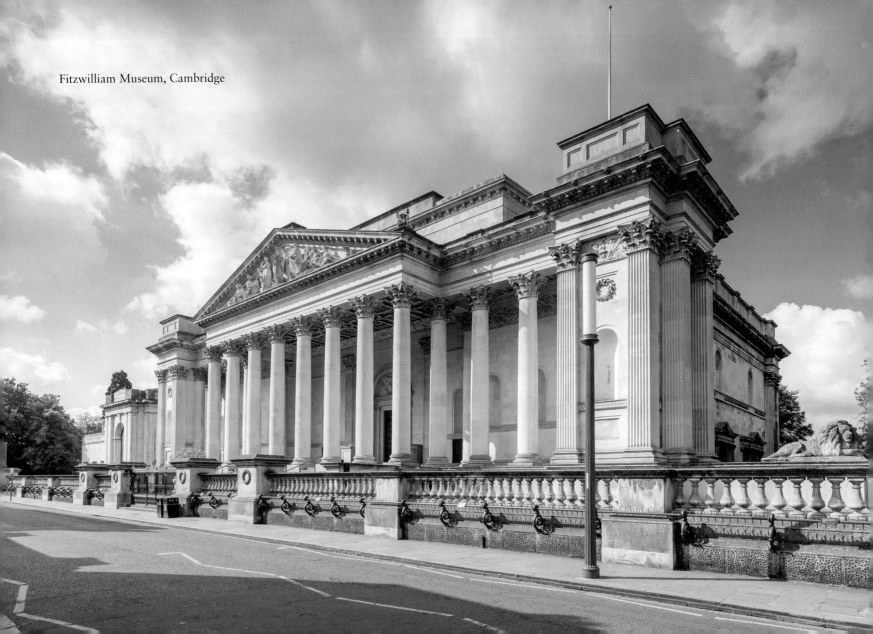

Fitzwilliam Museum, Cambridge

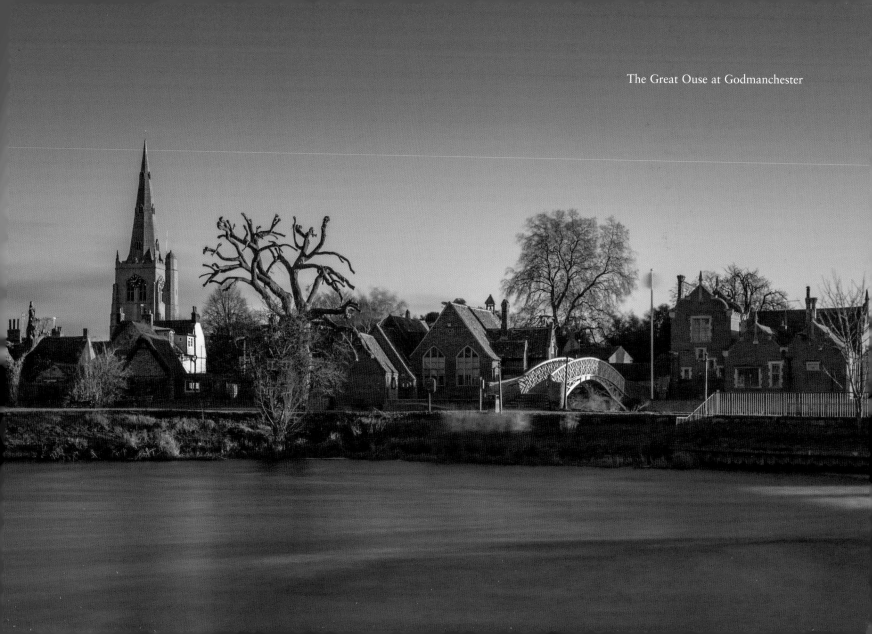

The Great Ouse at Godmanchester

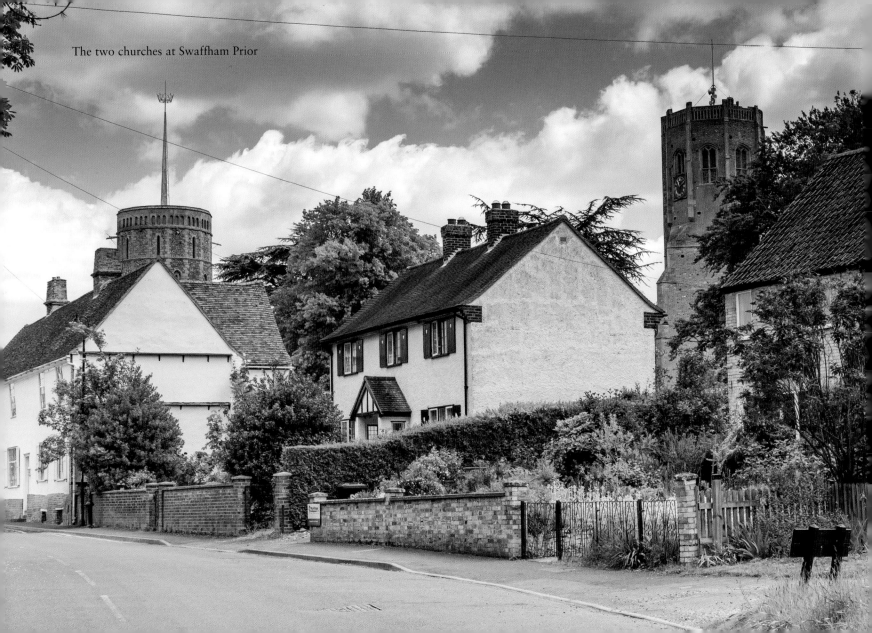

The two churches at Swaffham Prior

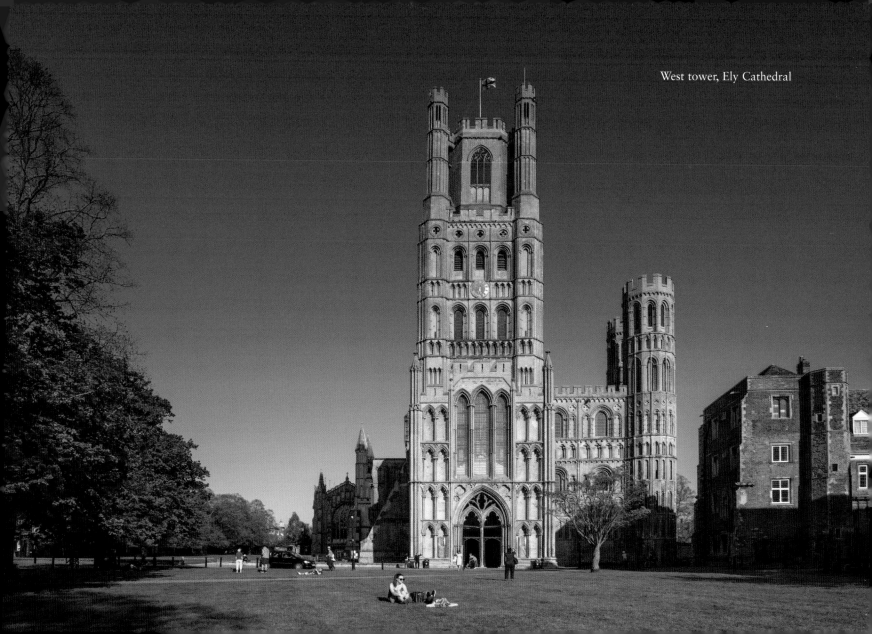

West tower, Ely Cathedral

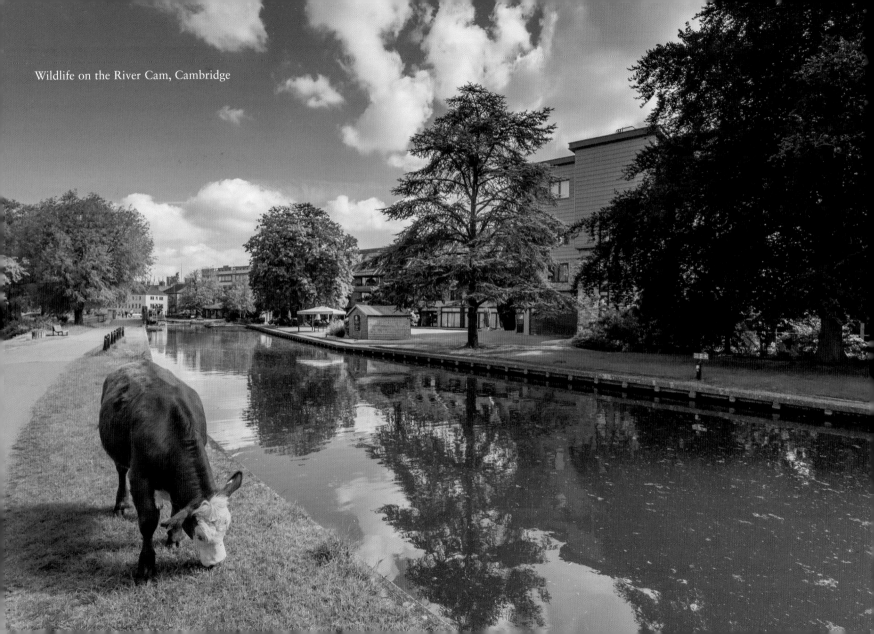

Wildlife on the River Cam, Cambridge